Walking with God

The Heart of True Spirituality

*Growing into balanced belief, authenticity of
personhood, and relational virtue—grounded in
childship of Christlikeness, and bearing fruit in
centered, integrated, becoming lifestyle discipleship—
lived obediently and practically over a lifetime*

Michael Phillips

GRANT STREET
PUBLISHERS

6-29-25

Walking with God

The Heart of True Spirituality

Note on notes: Footnoted references and brief clarifications are noted with numerals and are found at the bottom of each page. Endnotes of lengthier explanations and occasional digressions are noted with capital letters and are found at the end of the book.

> *"Noah was a righteous man...*
> *Noah walked with God."*
> *—Genesis 6:9*

Introduction

*"Noah was a righteous man...in his generation.
Noah walked with God."*
—Genesis 6:9

The title of this small compilation of reflections is obviously ambitious. My objective is not a thorough analysis of Christianity, but an overview of what I consider its essence.

This foundation undergirds my belief system and the authentic practical lifestyle I believe Christianity is meant to produce in its followers. Both of these—belief and lifestyle—as I have studied and reflected on them, emerge out of and mirror God's eternal purposes for his humanity. [A]

This overview will of necessity not include an apologetic for Christianity, examination of its doctrines, nor an extensive rationale in support of my conclusions. I have engaged in such discussions elsewhere. Those writings are readily available to anyone desirous of pursuing them. Neither will I attempt to justify my perspectives. I only lay them out and say, "This is the essence of my personal belief system as it has matured, developed, and come into focus over my lifetime. Thus, here I stand." [B]

The individual words of the lengthy subtitle are more far-reaching than the title itself. Their implications include nearly every aspect of life envisioned by serious Christians:

- Balanced belief.
- Authenticity of personhood.
- Relational virtue.
- Christlike childship.
- Centered, integrated, becoming lifestyle discipleship.
- Obedient practicality.

These eleven words—

- *Belief*
- *Authenticity*
- *Virtue*
- *Christlikeness*
- *Childship*
- *Centered*
- *Integrated*
- *Becoming*
- *Discipleship*
- *Obedience*
- *Practicality*

—woven in harmony into the fabric of character, I believe make vibrant world-changing Christianity, or *true spirituality*, possible in the day-to-day trenches of life where Christ's followers are meant to *walk with God.*

THREE WORDS

The final three words of that subtitle identify the underpinning strength that interlaces the eleven in a unity of purpose.

- *Over a lifetime.*

The lifelong unity of these principles, truths, and character qualities reveals my objective— both in my personal life and in this overview. It is a composite *full-life* quest. It comprises *all* these principles and truths.

Each of the eleven is deepened over time into the character of steadily maturing personhood.

Each one is infused into attitude, perspective, and behavior by ceaseless prayer, continual reaffirmation, daily practice, regular reorientation of purpose, and repetition of habit.

Hour by hour, day by day, year after year.

These are high spiritual goals. They do not become part of us all at once. They are spiritual aspirations—

- that we *grow into*…
- that we *mature* in our capacity to live…
- that we *think and pray diligently* about…
- that we *read and study* to understand…
- that we gradually *learn to practice*…
- and that the transforming grace of God's Spirit working within us *deepens into our characters.* [c]

They are principles, truths, habit patterns, and qualities of personal character that we *develop and cultivate*, and that God's Spirit infuses into us, over years and decades of walking with God.

The heart of spirituality is not comprised of a series of formulas, methods, or talking points that can be gleaned from a brief talk, the most analytically astute Bible study, or an insightful sermon. Nor will they be achieved by periodic bursts of enthusiasm, between which they are forgotten.

We're talking about *permanent*, unwavering hopes, purposes, aims, even *dreams* that define the kind of man or woman you and I desire to be and become.

HAND TO THE PLOW

The word "lifetime" may cause confusion. It is not delineated by the length or duration of one's walk with God—thirty years, fifty years, even

4

eighty years. Obviously the sooner one begins the better. Bad habit patterns of long duration that reflect self-centeredness rather than God-trusting, Spirit-yielding self-denial are harder to correct at fifty than twenty.

For my purpose I define "lifetime" beginning from the moment one decides:

- *"This* is the kind of life I want to live.
- *"This* is who I want to be.
- "I dedicate myself to practicing 24/7 lifestyle Christianity in every aspect of my life and relationships.
- "I will not compartmentalize my church, religious, so-called spiritual self as separate from other aspects of life.
- "Henceforth my life will be a unity.
- "It is my heart's desire to *walk with God.*
- "I commit to living as a *true* Christian, a disciple and follower of Jesus Christ.
- "I thus yield to God's Fathering, remaking, transforming, Christ-obeying ownership of my life."

For some that may indeed grow into a lifetime commitment of eighty years, for others twenty, for some perhaps five. Depending on how one theologically interprets the exchange, for the thief on the cross that *lifetime* might have been measured in but an hour or two.

The meaning would be conveyed better by adding the words, *There's no turning back.* Whatever duration of life lies ahead—whether measured in decades, years, or hours—that *lifetime* is one in which all facets of life are drawn into a concordant focus of purpose. Former outlooks are reevaluated and discarded. Life's priorities are remade.

Jesus enforced this perspective unequivocally when he said, "He who sets his hand to the plow and looks back is not fit for the kingdom of God."

That's when the *lifetime* begins—when we set our hands to the plow in obedience to Jesus' command, "Follow me." For one who wants to be fit for the kingdom of God, from that point on there's no turning back.

That's why counting the cost is such a vital component to discipleship. True spirituality is not to be entered into lightly. Walking with God is no frivolous undertaking.

Setting one's hand to the spiritual plow begins a "lifetime" process of growing, maturing, learning, practicing, developing, and cultivating the truths, principles, priorities, attitudes, habits, and outlook that are all drawn up into the lofty realm hinted at by the words *walking with God.*

Michael Phillips
Cullen, Scotland, 2024

1

Practicality

A code of personal character

Following the principle that the last shall be first, I begin with the last of the subtitle words listed on page 2: *Practicality.*

In my book *The Commands of Jesus,* I quoted a well-known theologian of the late twentieth century writing on the fundamental tenets of Christianity. He embarked on his discussion with a startling statement: "Christianity is not a code of conduct."

That simple sentence slammed into my head with magnum force. As he went on to discuss being "born again" and various doctrines of Christian "belief," including the necessity of "trusting Christ for salvation," that opening sentence remained seared on my brain.

I understand that he was emphasizing the truth that being a Christian involves more than simply "being a good person." Being a *Christ-ian* means literally being a "follower of Christ."

That means *following* him—doing what he said, heeding his example. It means being a *disciple.*

There is a heavy price tag to calling oneself a "disciple" of anyone. There's a cost. It's a serious word. It means following someone so completely that you attempt to model your life after his. It means pointing yourself in *his* direction, toward the direction *his* compass points, not a direction of your own.

So of course that author's statement is true as far as it goes. But *only* as far as it goes.

The more I reflected on it, I could not escape the conclusion that Christianity is *precisely* a code of conduct. Jesus taught behavior and attitudes, *not* a doctrinal belief system. Peruse the gospels with an eye to what Jesus actually told people to *do*. There's not much doctrine there. There's a lot of doctrine in Paul's writings, but not much in the gospels. Jesus did not primarily teach ideas or theology...he taught conduct, thought, and outlook.

Christianity *is* a code of attitude and behavior.

It is what we do, how we think, how we treat and think about others, and how we respond to God's Fatherhood in our moment-by-moment lives. It is a *code of personal character.*

Jesus laid out very succinctly and specifically what that code is. Then he told his listeners, "If you want to be my follower, if you want to be called my disciple, if you want to be identified with my name, if you want to walk with God as I walk with my Father...

"Do these things.

"Live by these principles.

"Think by these patterns.

"Believe these truths.

"Behave in these ways.

"You cannot walk with God and be my follower any other way than by adopting the code of conduct, thought, outlook, belief, and character that I am teaching you. To be *my* follower, you must do what I tell you. That's how you will become like me. That's how the world will know I came from the Father. That's how you will learn to walk with God."

That's why I begin with practicality rather than *belief*. It may surprise some for me to say that how we *live* and *behave*, how we *think* and what we *do*, and how we treat others, are more important than what we believe.

The heart of Christianity is not rooted in doctrine or theology…but in *practical life as it is lived*.

George MacDonald put it succinctly: "A man's real belief is that which he lives by…What a man believes, is the thing he does." [1]

In the four gospels of the New Testament, though of course we find many revolutionary ideas to empower it, the overarching theme is a call to *a code of character, conduct, attitude, behavior, and response*.

---

1 George MacDonald, *Unspoken Sermons, Second Series*, "The Truth in Jesus."

This is why I have devoted so much of my writing life to emphasizing the Bible's commands, and especially the commands of the Gospels. It is why I consider *The Commands of Jesus* the most important book I have ever written. Its 120 commands from the words of Jesus spell out with unmistakable practicality, clarity, and specificity the hallmarks of the code of character and life-outlook that define what being a Christian, a *follower*, is.

PRACTICALITY REINFORCED:
PAUL OF TARSUS AND THOMAS OF KEMPEN [2]

In *The Commands of Jesus*, I began my discussion of the Lord's commands with the simple command: *Love.*

It is the preeminent command of the Gospel, if not the whole Bible. To understand spirituality at all, *love* is the starting point. Not as a nebulous ideal, but as a practical way of life.

How can we turn this paramount command of Scripture, this imperative foundation of spirituality, into a daily reality?

By nearly any standard, 1 Corinthians 13 represents the summit of Paul's visionary wisdom into the nature of the love Jesus commands. Fifteenth century priest and monk Thomas

---

2 Thomas's years were 1379-1471. He is most commonly known as Thomas à Kempis, or simply Thomas Kempis.

Haemerken (German: Hämmerlein) of Kempen, in his classic *The Imitation of Christ*, echoes Paul with his own outline of love's attributes.

In placing these two Spirit-inspired lists side-by-side in conjunction with the commands of Jesus, we approach a remarkably practical definition of this code of character, attitude, and behavior. Plumbing the depths of these men's down-to-earth illumination of Jesus' love-commands sends us far along the road toward understanding what is meant by walking with God.

As will be familiar to most, Paul writes:

> *Love is patient and kind, not jealous or boastful, not arrogant or rude. Love does not insist on its own way, it is not irritable or resentful. It does not rejoice in wrong but rejoices in goodness and truth. Love bears all things, believes all things, hopes all things, endures all things.*

Fourteen hundred years later, Thomas Kempis added:

> *Love is active, sincere, affectionate; pleasant and amiable, courageous, patient, faithful, prudent, longsuffering, manly, and seeks not her own...Love is circumspect, humble and upright...nor attending to vain things. It is sober, chaste, steady, quiet, and guarded in all the senses.*

Please do not be put off by his use of the word *manly*, or ask why I do not modify it in keeping with progressive orthodoxy. The word simply means strong, vigorous, and muscular of virtue.

I would like to challenge whomever happens to read these words, as I challenge myself, when we are alone and in a thoughtful frame of heart, to consider these noteworthy character qualities in light of sensible, concrete, relational, balanced, lifestyle spirituality.

Put aside briefly thoughts of the *ideas* of Christianity. Consider instead a simple revolutionary proposition:

Might the attributes of attitude and character set down by our brothers Paul and Thomas—lived daily in how we think and respond to those who cross our path—go far to identify the characteristics that make one a practically loving and gospel-obedient disciple of Jesus?

What if we were to say, *One who walks with God is:*

- Patient
- Kind
- Not jealous
- Not boastful
- Not arrogant
- Not rude
- Not irritable
- Not resentful

- Active
- Sincere
- Affectionate
- Pleasant
- Amiable
- Courageous
- Patient
- Faithful
- Prudent
- Longsuffering
- Manly
- Circumspect
- Humble
- Upright
- Not attending to vain things
- Sober
- Chaste
- Steady
- Quiet
- Guarded in all the senses.

and then add that he or she:

- Does not insist on his own way
- Does not rejoice in wrong
- Rejoices in goodness and truth
- Bears all things

- Believes all things
- Hopes all things
- Endures all things
- Seeks not her own.

Rather than a list of *beliefs*, what if these qualities and responses comprised the standard—judging by observed personal character—by which the world determined who was and who was not a follower of Christ?

If these virtues, traits, practices, behaviors, and habits are indeed defining characteristics of love, practically lived in the body of Christ and in the world, this is *exactly* the standard Jesus lays out in John 13:35 for determining how the world evaluates who is a Christian.

"By this will all men know that you are my disciples, if you have love for one another."

Not a word about correct doctrine as defining how discipleship will be known, heaven or hell, the cross, the blood, the trinity, the resurrection, being born again, trusting Christ for salvation, repentance, a sinner's prayer, or church [3]...only the powerful four words *if you have love*.

This is the *practicality* of Christianity from Jesus' own lips.

---

3   All these, and much more, *are* of course emphasized by Jesus elsewhere, but not in *this* context as imperative in his final message to his disciples.

2
Belief

Three essential truths in which
Christianity is anchored

Yet Christianity *is* a belief system.

It is comprised of *ideas*, even what we might call *theological* ideas. Some of these ideas are more important than others, but none are insignificant. To walk with God we have to understand who is the God we're attempting to walk with, and what are his purposes for the men and women who walk with him.

To know, understand, and walk with God thus requires accurate *belief* about him and *in* him.

I said earlier that the attributes listed by Paul and Thomas Kempis may go a long way to help illuminate what love means. But they do not go *all* the way in defining walking with God.

They provide a foundation—clear from Jesus' words in John 13:35—but are not enough in themselves to *fully* define the discipleship of true spirituality.

Being a good person is not enough *in itself*. Upon the foundation of practical character must be built the house of Christian discipleship. The walls and rooms and roof of that house are constructed by the *belief system* and *ideas* (even doctrines, though I do not care for the term) of the Christian faith.

Many believe that the *ideas* of the Christian faith come first as the foundation, and that lifestyle discipleship, personal character, and virtue such as evidenced in the two love-lists from the last chapter, are built upon those beliefs. From this perspective, it is the ideas and beliefs that lead to and *produce* virtue, character, and practically visible discipleship.

Of course this is true. As we mature in belief, the qualities of character should be manifested in how we live. The tree of belief grows the fruit of character goodness and virtue. All those attributes listed earlier, as well as foundational, also represent the goodness-fruits of a belief system anchored in truth and lived practically. Paul calls them the "fruit of the Spirit."

It is unimportant to argue the relative sequence of primacy between belief and practicality. *Both* are primary and foundational. *Neither* comes first. They intertwine so completely they cannot be separated at all.

As is true of all elements of faith, they function like the two blades of a pair of scissors. They work together or they don't work at all.

Such is the wonderful unity between *faith* and *obedience,* between *ideas* and *practice,* between *character* and *belief.* The themes that make up the chapters of this book form a unity. All function in interconnected harmony.

If one prefers a different sequence, interchange *Practicality* and *Belief.* I am equally comfortable envisioning belief as the foundation and practicality of attitude and behavior as the walls and roof of the house of spirituality.

I don't care which blade of the scissors any of us pick up first. As long as we pick up both, and use them together. [D]

ESSENTIALS OF CHRISTIAN BELIEF

To attempt a thorough discussion of Christian "belief" is obviously not my intent. Thousands of books, entire *series* of books thousands of pages long, "systematic theologies" by the hundreds, have been written over the centuries, from Augustine to Calvin right up to our own time. Catholic, Orthodox, Evangelical and every persuasion between has its *own* doctrinal systematic theology.

I would contend that the majority of them have influenced the world very little toward walking-with-God, discipleship Christianity. Many have done more harm than good by their failure to promote understanding of and daily

17

response to the Fatherhood of God as that Fatherhood was illuminated into the world by Jesus. Most of those myriad theologies will be revealed in the light of eternity to have been little more than religious wood, hay, and stubble that will be consumed by Malachi's furnace and thankfully forgotten.

What then are the beliefs that *will* be revealed by that eternal fire to have been the true gold upon which Christlike walking-with-God discipleship is built?

What are the beliefs that will *endure*?

What are the beliefs that produce and grow the fruit of the Spirit and a virtuous lifestyle of discipleship and character?

What are Christianity's essential beliefs taught in the Gospel by Jesus?

To answer this important question requires a brief trip down memory lane. At the end of that detour, some of more doctrinal bent will insist on adding dozens, if not hundreds, of specifics to my list of essentials.

Nevertheless, I stand by the simplicity of the conviction this experience early in my walk confirmed to me, and which has remained unshaken ever since.

THE CHALLENGE...THE COMMANDS

Not long after my wife Judy and I were married, our pastor challenged me to go to the

New Testament for the answer to a matter about which he and I disagreed. Not long afterward I spent a week alone in a cheap motel some 300 miles from home. I took with me only my typewriter, two favorite Bibles, and paper, pens, and pencils. No books. No commentaries. No concordance.

I decided to broaden my inquiry beyond the issue my pastor and I had tussled over, and try instead to isolate *all* the New Testament's commands. At that point I was not interested in doctrines or beliefs or opinions, neither mine nor his. I wanted to know what the Bible commands Christians to *do*.

The issue prompting the search was no mere doctrine. It was intensely practical. Whatever I discovered could well change the focus of Judy's and my daily and weekly lives, as well as many of our relationships.

It was *very* personal. I was in search of what I, Mike Phillips and no one else, believed and was commanded to do.

On the morning of my first day I opened my Bible to Matthew 1:1, placed a blank sheet of paper in my typewriter, and started through the New Testament. The initial entry on the top of the paper did not come until Matthew's third chapter. The words originated out of the mouth of John the Baptist. From the second verse of that chapter, I typed out the first direct command to be found in the New Testament, "Repent, for the kingdom of heaven is near."

I continued on with my list. Several days later I reached the end of *Revelation*. By then my list was forty-four pages long.

That week's study changed my life. I knew I had touched the heart of God's instructions to man about how we are meant to live. I knew I had laid hold of the anchoring purpose of Jesus' mission, the core and foundation of Christianity, the daily mechanics of discipleship, the basis of fulfillment and purpose in life, the origin of wholeness of personhood, the lifeblood of relationships, even the essence of who God is and what are his eternal purposes for his creation, his universe, and his people.

These realizations did not come fully formed all at once. I continued to study and reflect on the commands, synthesizing and categorizing, differentiating between direct and indirect and implied commands, prioritizing the commands of Jesus above commands that came from others, and distinguishing between *universal* commands intended for all humanity (*Love your neighbor as yourself...do unto others as you would have them do unto you...do good to those who mistreat you*) and those that were intended only for a moment of time to those involved in the gospel story (*Give me a drink...stretch out your hand...come here*).

The commands became a lifetime study. Out of it emerged the conviction that Christianity was not primarily about ideas, beliefs, doctrine, theology, salvation, blessing, baptism, church membership, church teaching, faith, heaven, hell, prophecy, the sacraments, justification, fellowship, sanctification, being born again, worship, speaking in tongues, prayer, or what is meant by the trinity. All these are important, but I realized they were *secondary* aspects of Christianity.

At its rock bottom foundation, I knew more clearly than ever that Christianity was a way of life, not a set of ideas. Its distilled essence was embodied in how we *live*, and whether or not we live by God's commands.

I came to recognize that the Bible's commands, and preeminently the commands of Jesus in the four gospels, represent what I call "the true North of God's compass." They point in the direction he intends men and women to walk as they make their way through life.

In the commands I knew I had discovered the heart of spirituality.

Because my perspective of what constitutes the central ideas of Christianity have emerged out of the New Testament's commands, and are lived and personalized by obedience to the commands, my summary of those *central ideas* form a very different list of Christian fundamentals than is found in most books on Christian doctrine or heard from any pulpit.

Two books on my shelf, by two of the most highly touted evangelical theologians of our time—boasting that their books comprise the "essentials" of the Christian faith—give ninety-four and one-hundred-and-one doctrines their authors consider required for an understanding of Christianity.

My list of imperative truths contains only three.

THREE PILLARS OF BELIEF

I do not call my threefold list of essentials doctrines, but *truths* that point to the nature and substance of who God is, and what are his eternal purposes in the universe. The many doctrines of Christianity are subsumed and incorporated *into* these three high truths. [E]

They are *Fatherhood*, *Christlikeness*, and *obedience*.

ONE: The first essential and foundational truth Jesus taught was a simple yet profoundly life-changing one—*the divine Fatherhood.*

God is mankind's Father. This has always been a revolutionary truth—and mankind has been obtusely stubborn to acknowledge it. Contrary to millennia of false imaginings that continue in our own time, Jesus taught that God was an infinitely good, loving, kind, trustworthy, and forgiving Father, whose desire is only good for the men and women of his creation. He will never cease the attempt to do them good, even beyond death if necessary.

This may seem like a doctrinal or theological concept. In fact, it is the most practical truth we will ever encounter. If God is infinitely good and loving, more loving than can be imagined, our *true* Father who is more a father to us than any earthly father could ever be, that resounding truth changes everything we have wrongly been taught.

It turns upside-down what most people— Christians and non-Christians alike—persist in wrongly believing about God.

Furthermore, for Christians it *has* to be true because Jesus told us so:

God is your Father, and I am a reflection of him. He is just like me. I and the Father are one.

Upon the foundation of the goodness of divine Fatherhood is built everything that comprises what we call Christianity. This is *the* primary essential belief of the Christian faith.

Without the infinite goodness of God's eternal Fatherhood, there is no Christianity.

TWO: The second foundational truth Jesus taught was equally revolutionary—the truth of *childship Christlikeness.*

In addition to telling his followers to do what he told them—to obey his commands—over and over Jesus reinforced the truth that, the Father being the Father, he was the *Son.*

23

He was the *child* of his good and loving Father.

He was subservient to the Father. His own will was nothing. His only will was to do the will of his Father—to obey his Father.

He taught the truth of perfect childship—his *own* childship as a Son of his Father. With a good and loving and perfect Father, what else could a child desire than to obey? The delight of Jesus was in being a perfect Son by obeying his Father.

Then he told his followers, in essence, *I want you to be happy, whole, fulfilled, obedient children just like me. You are my brothers and sisters and God is our Father. Be his children and become like me. Live in the eternal childship of the Father. Let all the goodness of the Father's nature flow into your life by living as he tells mankind to live, by obeying him. Be his sons and daughters.*

These words I have imagined from the mouth of Jesus are a command, an invitation, and a promise. Obeying the command, accepting the invitation, and entering into the fulfillment of the promise, reveal the eternal purpose of God throughout his creation and in the lives of every man, woman, and child who ever lived and ever will live.

That high purpose is *Christlikeness*. Obviously Jesus himself didn't use that word. He did, however, embody its principle in everything he taught his disciples about childship. All the doctrines about the life and death of Jesus—the incarnation, the cross, the resurrection, and many other important aspects of his life—are understood in their fullness as they illuminate the high truth of his eternal Sonship. The childship informs all the rest. The centrality of the cross in Christian belief is rooted in the centrality of the Lord's Sonship.

In hundreds of ways Jesus was constantly trying to convey, *Imitate me, do as I do, think as I think, love as I love, respond to the Father as I respond to him, treat people as I do, lay down your lives as I lay down mine.*

The purpose of God throughout creation and throughout eternity is to grow and develop sons and daughters—you and me!—who will mature throughout their earthly lives and the next, into beings who reflect the very nature of his firstborn Son—sons and daughters who become like Jesus.

This supreme purpose, as C.S. Lewis says, will not be completed in this life.[4] But it is God's intent that we move steadily toward it. That is why he has given us his compass—to point us toward the North of Christlikeness.

In the Bible's commands, he has given us very clear instructions how to follow that compass toward that North of his eternal purpose.

THREE: This brings us to my third imperative truth of the Christian walk of faith—*obedience*.

---

4 In *Mere Christianity*, chapter entitled "Counting the Cost."

The commands are the mechanism by which God's Spirit grows the Lord's followers into his sons and daughters who gradually, over a lifetime, come to reflect the nature and character, the attitudes and behavior, the motives and responses, and the eternal perspective of Jesus.

This is the ultimate goodness, fulfillment, and fruitfulness of life. It was for this purpose that Jesus came. Obedience to his commands is the doorway into the Christlikeness which is God's purpose and our eternal destiny.

These, then, are the threefold pillars of my belief system as a Christian man. In my view, these essential truths comprise the priorities, worldview, life-perspective, and marching orders of those committed to 24/7 lifestyle Christian discipleship.

- The Infinite Goodness of God's Fatherhood.

- Childship Christlikeness.

- Command Obedience.

It will be obvious that the doctrine, theology, church activity, experientialism, and ministry which consume the focus, practice, finances, and obsession of the majority of Christendom miss this three-way bull's eye of practical faith almost entirely. When was the last time you heard a sermon preached on any of these? If you have heard one recently, then you are of the small fortunate minority to have a pastor or priest who understands the primacy of the commands.

Whatever, however subtly and seemingly harmlessly—

- repudiates the infinite goodness of God's Fatherhood with doctrines and belief systems inconsistent with that infinite goodness...

- does not urge, challenge, and lead to obedience to the Bible's commands...

- and thus does not produce practical Christlikeness of discipleship-character...

—will, along with most of man's systematic theologies and spurious religious teachings, be revealed as wood, hay, and stubble in the end.

We have to know God *accurately* if we hope to engage personally with the daily imperative of his divine Fatherhood in our lives. To know him accurately, we have to know his nature and eternal purposes.

God's intent in each of our lives is that we grow into his obedient sons and daughters of increasingly selfless Christlike childship. The heart of true spirituality is rooted in the life desire and prayer to model oneself after the character of Jesus. Such is God's eternal purpose for us all.

Living in obedience to the commands of Jesus, and other biblical commands that harmonize with and amplify the foundational commands of the four gospels, represents the bull's eye of practical faith, the essence of daily walking-with-God Christianity.

3
Christlikeness

Make me like Jesus

More than fifty years ago I began asking God to do something in my life. The consequences of that prayer I did not foresee.

SECONDARY OR PRIMARY?

During the years since, I have watched many Christians become preoccupied with the externals and blessings of religious experience. They are encouraged by self-aggrandizing pastors and teachers to pray in the *power of the flesh* for temporal blessing rather than in the *spirit of Christ* for Godliness of character.

It is possible to pray for things of *secondary* significance, and then, interpreting events that may have nothing to do with the working of God's Spirit as answers to those prayers, wrongly assume that God's will has been accomplished.

As a result of false teachings that take advantage of this immature lust for blessing, few ask what is God's *primary* will for his people?

What is it that God wants to do in your life and mine above *all* other things?

What is the *summum bonum,* the "supreme good" of life—the ultimate purpose that is in God's mind and heart when he thinks of *you* and *me?*

SONS AND DAUGHTERS

That supreme thing can be simply stated: That we become sons and daughters of God who are conformed to the image of Christ.

Jesus was *the* Son of God, the "only begotten" Son. God's design is that we also become sons and daughters, Jesus' younger brothers and sisters, who are *like* him—who love like him, think as he thought, know God's Fatherhood as he knew it, respond like him, resist the enemy like him, treat people as he would, trust our mutual Father as he did, deny ourselves as he did, and who daily pray with him in the garden, "Not my will, but yours be done."

We will never be like him in his perfection, but we *are* to become like him in attitude, thought, and motive. This is God's *preeminent* purpose in the humanity of his creation.

Obviously this is a lifelong process. We *don't* love or think or respond or trust God like Jesus did. But to turn us into the kind of people who *can* do so—with infinitesimal baby steps at first, then growing steadily more capable of it as our lives

30

progress—is the whole point of Christianity. There is nothing else the Christian life is about.

We will never attain this high objective perfectly in this life. But it is toward this end that God is leading us, and toward this divine "center" of being that the prayer of Christlikeness aims us.

Such a transformation into men and women that reflect the nature of Jesus Christ cannot be accomplished externally. God wants more than mere believers. He wants more than people who can parrot back doctrinally correct spiritual phrases. What is in his heart to accomplish will not come about by outward manifestation. It happens inwardly, as we become people of a certain nature. He is involved in the enterprise of fashioning eternally noble, righteous sons and daughters.

At whatever point any man or woman—in the midst of a sinful and selfish nature, whatever his or her past—relinquishes self-will and places that will into God's hands to be remade—and to the extent such an individual yields to the miraculous, transforming, remaking process—the Spirit of God begins to fashion a son or daughter who will one day bear the image and reflect the nature of his firstborn Son.

The request I mentioned earlier when I began asking God to conform me to the image of his Son was in the form of a prayer:

"God, make me like Jesus."

I call this the prayer of Christlikeness. It is not a prayer to be prayed nonchalantly. Counting the cost is imperative. There is a heavy price to Christlikeness.

One who doesn't mean business with God will only slow his spiritual progress by praying it casually. The words of the prayer seem simple enough. But the means by which it is answered are anything but simple.

The prayer of Christlikeness represents the ultimate road less travelled. It is a prayer that begins a pilgrimage that, if undertaken seriously and reaffirmed regularly, will change everything. It sets us on a course apart from the crowd, even the "spiritual" crowd. In quiet and subtle ways the pray-er of this prayer will find himself diverging from many former associations. A singular and uncommon journey has begun that cannot be fathomed by most in the religious multitude.

I was young when I began praying the prayer of Christlikeness. I was incapable of counting the cost. Where it would lead, I had no idea. There have been occasional moments since when I have faced such depths of discouragement, even despair, that I have come within a hair's breadth of taking it back, of shouting, "God, forget it...I still believe, but I no longer want to pay the price of praying to become like Jesus. I no longer want to endure the road to the cross!"

At such times I have been conscious of standing before a cliff of spiritual decision, poised to jump, reminded of our Lord's second and third temptations in Matthew 4. But each time I have stepped back and in tears of anguish have reaffirmed the prayer, though there have been times when it has been so difficult that my stomach physically ached to do so.

The prayer of Christlikeness is no prayer for the spiritually fainthearted. At such times, it has not been *strength* that has overcome the urge to recant. When I say this prayer is not for the spiritually fainthearted, I do not mean the strong and confident and self-assured.

I am not strong. It has been pure determination to see it through that has driven me back to my knees in tears, again to reaffirm—in my *weakness*, not my strength: "Father...whatever it takes...I am willing...create in me the heart of a true son...and make me like Jesus."

It is difficult to see much headway over the years. Sometimes it is very difficult to say the words. It is a quiet and lonely prayer, a sacrificial and humbling prayer, an invisible prayer, a prayer that scrapes at the sores and scabs of self, a prayer that exposes the ugliness of what I see when I look in the mirror.

Some may ask if it is presumptuous to pray the prayer of Christlikeness.

Not if prayed in recognition of the human weakness implicit in the very words.

My failure is implied by the prayer itself. I pray it *because* I will never reach anything close to Christlikeness in this life.

Paul wrote: "Not that I have already obtained all this, or have already been made perfect, but I press on to take hold of that for which Christ Jesus took hold of me...I press on toward the goal..." (Philippians 3:12-14)

That is what the prayer represents—pressing on toward the *summit* of God's purpose.

NO MAGIC WAND

The prayer of Christlikeness is not a prayer that can be answered with a divine magic wand. God doesn't work that way. He works slowly, through process, through the human will, through growth, through events, through decisions, and through motive.

He answers the prayer of Christlikeness through *our* willingness to become self-denying sons and daughters, through *our* dedication to that ongoing growth process, and by the empty hands of our *own* obedience.

God cannot answer the prayer on his own, without my taking an equal share in the process. To enable God to answer the prayer:

- I recognize God's eternal purpose to grow sons and daughters of Christlikeness, understanding this to be his purpose for *me*.

- Acknowledging him as my Creator and Father, I choose to place myself under the obligation and imperative to fall in with that purpose.

- I dedicate myself to his remaking of me in the image of Christ.

- I thus join him by doing what he has given me to do toward that end.

We are not *made* like Jesus, we must *become* like Jesus.

Change comes slowly. It comes as tiny urgings of the *self-nature* are ignored, denied, relinquished, and refused admission to life's throne-room of decision, so that the *Christ-nature* can rule in place of them.

The more of *self* that is cut away, vanquished, and put to death as a source of motive, attitude, thought, response, and choice, the more I am able to place in the hands of Jesus to allow him to set my motive, attitude, thought, response, and choice.

We can pray the prayer of Christlikeness all our lives, however, and nothing will happen by simply laying on the operating table, passively expecting God to accomplish the cutting away of self. This is what many Christians are taught—that God works a transformation within believers by a magical surgery called sanctification.

But there is no magic in God's economy. He does not cut away unkindness, resentment, unforgiveness, covetousness, jealousy, irritability, impatience, lust, and self-centeredness by himself.

In praying, "Make me like Jesus," you and I join the surgical team. The tool used to answer the prayer is not a single-bladed scalpel of miracle, but a double-handled pair of spiritual scissors that is used in the moment-by-moment trenches of life.

They are the scissors of command and obedience.

How this spiritually miraculous surgical tool functions—gradually putting self to death, steadily vanquishing its influence from motive, attitude, thought, and action—is one of the least apprehended aspects of the walk of faith. We must wield one handle, God holds the other.

Christlikeness is a *mutually*-effected eternal objective shared between ourselves and the Spirit of God.

4

Childship

Father, what would you have me do?

Dedicating oneself to the prayer of Christlikeness begins a lifetime of growth. At whatever point one first prays it, and *means* it to the deepest marrow of the will—whether at fifteen or eighty-five—all priorities, motives, attitudes, ambitions, and perspectives begin to be refashioned according to different parameters.

Life's foundation has shifted. Orientations turned upside-down. Perspectives and priorities once cherished as equally vital to existence as breathing are now seen as stale and profitless.

Some of these changes are immediate and sweep over and through us with new winds of purpose. We feel caught up and carried along in spite of ourselves. This is especially true when we are young and full of excitement in our walks with God.

Most of the changes, however, are silent, invisible, and slow to materialize.

WHAT REALLY IS SPIRITUAL GROWTH?

Spiritual growth is one of the most commonly recognized components of the Christian life. In connection with the prayer of Christlikeness, however, we are speaking of something vastly different than the accumulation of spiritual data that often goes by that name.

Many Christians define *growth* by an increase in their storehouses of biblical and doctrinal knowledge accompanied by expanding insights into spiritual principles. The "old man" delights in filling those soul-granaries to overflowing.

What *Make-me-like-Jesus* disciples consider growth, rather, is toward *less* of anything to which their flesh can cling, take pleasure in, or feed on. Whatever exalts and nourishes the *self* is a step backward rather than forward. Increasing *knowledge* about the Bible and doctrine and theology, in particular, when kept in the head rather than feeding the inner man, is admirably suited for nourishing and exalting the old Adam.

When one begins praying the prayer of Christlikeness, he or she is no longer his own. Every motive gradually becomes imbued with new significance, new perspective, new subtleties. To respond as Jesus responded steals imperceptibly by degrees into consciousness as the illuminating purpose giving everything in life revised definition and meaning.

The word *gradually* is imperative. All growth is slow. It takes *time* for seeds to sprout and for tiny root fibers to reach down into the earth. Expecting too much too soon is a prescription for endless discouragement.

Growth begins with motive. The *desire* to grow animates the seed into life. It sprouts, roots deepen, and fruit will grow as long as the motive and *desire* to grow continues to water the fragile but increasingly robust plant of obedience.

I had originally written the sentence three paragraphs above, "To respond as Jesus responded *floods* into being…"

I realized that, except in brief moments, that is not an accurate image of what happens. We are not usually flooded with new outlooks. Rather, we slowly become aware that they are slipping in the back door, invisibly changing perspectives and priorities. We may not even be aware of these subtle changes in our outlook at first.

THE PRAYER OF CHILDSHIP

From the prayer of Christlikeness, the practical question arises: How is it to be done, this high and holy thing? How can we, in any true sense, actually respond, behave, think…*like Jesus?* Is it even possible?

Astonishingly, the answer is yes.

We can be like him in the most important of ways in which he lived his own Sonship. We can turn our hearts to the Father. With Jesus we can say, *Father, what would you have me do?*

This is what I call "the prayer of childship." With this prayer of chosen subservience, we make ourselves one with Jesus.

It is clear that Jesus did not need to pray for Christlikeness. He *was* Christ—the Son of God. The truth of it was alive in his essential being.

But what made him Christlike? Of what was his Christness comprised? What made him a Son?

The answer lies in the question itself. He was the obedient *Son* of the perfect *Father*.

This means neither more nor less than this:

Jesus was a *child*.

He *did* pray the prayer of childship. He did what his Father wanted him to do. He took his Father's will into himself. He replaced his own will with that greater Father-will.

In the example of that childness we discover our own doorway into the childness of Christlikeness.

A CHOSEN CHILDSHIP

The most startling aspect of the gospel story is that Jesus was not forced into his role in the divine drama that resulted in the world's salvation.

He *chose* his Sonship.

Jesus' childship was not automatic. It didn't just happen. He had to choose the submission of his way to the Father's will, just as we do. He *decided* to submit his will. He confronted this decision not just once or twice, but ten thousand times, over and over...every day...all his life.

Though modernism despises the word, the prayer of childness is a prayer of *submission*.

Jesus was not a perfect Son because he could not help it. In the midst of a fully human mortality, he *chose* to be a child. His every breath, every thought, every action, was both a praying and a living out of the prayer—*Father, what would you have me do?*

NO ANGEL

Lurking between the lines of much Christian doctrine is an angel-Jesus—a being without the same kind of free will we have...a half-man, half-angel at the center of the gospel story.

But Jesus was born a *complete* man, with the fully developed free will of humanity. No halo glowed above his head. His was a physical and mortal body. His was a human will. He got tired. He sweat. He went to the bathroom. He had to wash his hair and his hands and his feet. His brain possessed the capacity to think. He had emotions. He loved. He became irritated at his disciples and angry at the Pharisees. He felt fear for what he had to face as the cross neared.

This was no glow-in-the-dark Son of God whose Sonship came any other way than ours must come. He was a Son because he *chose* to be a Son.

In truth he was God-man, the Divine Man. Yet we mustn't obscure the totality of his manhood by embellishing his divinity. We can't imagine that his Father smuggled a tiny magic wand into the manger at Bethlehem for his Son to pull out when the going got rough—to make sure no stain of sin got too close, no temptation bit too dangerously deep.

Mary held no cute little baby angel in her arms who was *incapable* of sin.

The enormity of Christ's Saviorhood is found in this—that it is born out of a manhood that *chose* to be our redeemer. Mary held a fully human *baby* in the swaddling clothes of the incarnation...*her* own son, and *God's* own Son.

Then Jesus grew in wisdom and in stature and in favor with God and man. As he grew he continually humbled himself, emptied himself, living out the full expression of what childship entails in the practicalities of life. He learned childship progressively—first as Joseph's son, and then, as his childship took on more eternal significance, as God's Son.

Urged every second to exalt self, only a mortal can *choose* self-relinquishing childship.

No angel can make that choice. That's why God did not send an angel merely to *announce* the kingdom of God. He sent his Son to show us *how to live* in that kingdom.

We had to do more than just *hear* the message. We had to *see* it. We had to know it could be done, that the mortal will of self could submit itself to the higher Will of our Creator and Father.

An angel might have been able to *tell* us. Only a man could *show* us.

So God became a man.

Not a pretend man or a partial man. but a *real* man.

FREE WILL—THE MECHANISM OF CHILDSHIP

Yet the half-angel image is hard to exorcise from our perceptions. We imagine that it was *easier* for Jesus to lay down his will than it is for us. But as Jesus grew and matured, his will was a fully *human* will. He *wanted* his own way. Our struggles were his struggles.

No sin exists in wanting one's way. The choice that follows determines *child-ship* or *self-ship*. Jesus did not enter into the fullness of Sonship in Bethlehem. His abandonment of self-rule required the *real* blood, the *real* sweat, and the *real* tears of genuine manhood. He *became* a Son by the exercise of his free will.

The *will* is the deepest, strongest thing we possess as human beings. Our power of volition is our link with God himself. It is God's creative fingerprint stamped within each one of us.

Think what God did. He created beings that were both *like* him, and yet at the same time

43

separate from him. So separate, in fact, as to be capable of choosing or *not* choosing to walk in relationship with him.

The marvel of the thing continually overwhelms me, that God placed free will in the center of creation.

Free will is simply the most remarkable aspect of creation. It is *completely* our own. For having given it, God in a sense bound the hands of his own omnipotence to interfere with it. What each of us does with this priceless possession of volition—the power to choose—is the great drama of eternity.

THE HIGHEST EXERCISE OF FREE WILL

Naturally, then, comes the question: What is the *highest* choice the will can make?

It is this: To *yield* it.

The highest is always to *give*. It is why the most far-reaching love involves sacrifice. To *give* most deeply always means giving *oneself*.

"For God so loved the world that he gave..."

To *give*, to *yield*, to *give away*, even to *relinquish* and *give up*...these are the ingredients of the highest forms of love we know.

We return, then, to the *will*. Not just any "will," an abstract will...but *your* will and *my* will. What is the highest, the deepest, the ultimate thing we can each do with this gift we have been given.

Yield it...*abandon* it...*sacrifice* it...and *give* it back to our Creator and Father who gave it to us in the first place.

We know this is the highest because it is exactly this yielding we witness in the life of Jesus.

The *will* is the most individual element of our complex humanity. To give it *back* to the Creator, yielding it again into his hands, represents the *perfect* expression of human freedom. In such a self-willed abandonment of the right to self-rule we reach the crowning apex of human personhood.

Having achieved adulthood, mature manhood and womanhood, to then *give up* our right to them, to lay them down for the *greater* privilege of becoming children again, is in the world's eyes folly.

In the economy of God's kingdom, it is the path to the Christlikeness that is our eternal destiny.

GETHSEMANE—THE DANGEROUS CLIMAX OF THE GOSPEL

We now approach holy ground, the pinnacle of what human life can, should, and was intended to mean. In the faintly visible impressions of the Lord's knees in Gethsemane our own childship is birthed.

When Jesus entered the depths of Gethsemane, he carried one possession with him. That was the same free will that God had given to Adam's race in Eden, the same free will you and I possess.

I maintain, perhaps controversially, that the climax of the gospel, the very apex of Jesus' mission on earth, came in the garden's deep silences with his prayer, "Not my will."

The implication of the Lord's chosen childship—*Not my will Father...what would you have me do?*— is perhaps greater than we realize.

Whenever true choice exists, complete *free* will, then decisions can go either way. Two answers always lay before the man or woman with free will—*This* vs. *that*...to the *right* or the *left*...go *forward* or turn *back*...*yes* or *no*...*my* will or the will of *another*.

Think what this means. Jesus' decisions, too, could have gone either way.

Could he have failed? Could he have chosen self-will rather than God's will? Does the question ring with blasphemous doubt of his divinity?

We mustn't be fearful to ask God high things. The most probing questions force us deep into the realities of our faith. If we are unwilling to make the prayer of childship *real*, stripping it of pious gloss, it is pointless to pray it.

Father, what would you have me do? has no meaning unless there is a *self-will* and a *Father-will*...and unless the freedom exists to choose either.

To the very cross Jesus' fully functioning human will remained alive. At any point he could have said to his Father, "I want your will no longer. I hereby call an end to this mission. I'm my own man now."

I believe, therefore, that Jesus *could* have failed. He did not *have* to choose the Father-will. That's why I call Gethsemane a *dangerous* climax to the gospel. When Jesus entered Gethsemane's depths, the fate of the world hung in the balance. The divine risk of free will had reached its pinnacle—mind-bending as it is to say it—in the person of God himself.

The Creator of free will found himself staring face to face into the mirror of his own creation, weighing in the depths of the humanity he had imposed upon himself, the full implications of his creation.

What if Jesus had not added the final words to his *If it be possible*? What if instead he had crept out of the garden while the disciples were asleep, returned to Galilee, and gone into hiding?

That he did not do so, that he knelt and whispered the thunderous history-changing words, *Not my will,* makes the Saviorhood of his divine Sonship all the more precious.

CHILDSHIP IS BIRTHED IN GETHSEMANE

It is an incredible thing that the Founder of our faith conquered sin by emptying himself of self. What an unexpected weapon to deal the death blow to sin—self-denial.

47

Peter drew the sword and would fight sin by might. Judas would attempt to manipulate the divine will into an earthly mission against Rome's rule

But not the perfect Son.

"Put away your sword, Peter," says Jesus. "Do not lay up for yourself treasures on earth, Judas. My Father's kingdom functions by different rules. I will conquer, not with worldly power, but in the simplicity of childship."

After twenty centuries, many of the Lord's followers are still seduced by the examples of Peter and Judas that night in the garden, seeking to change the world by might and by money, by the power of the sword and the power of the purse. There is only one way to change the world. Yet it is the one thing God's people have steadfastly *not* done.

- It is easy to proclaim the gospel. It is difficult to die to self.

- It serves the flesh to draw the sword. It is difficult to lay down the sword.

- It is easy to preach. It is difficult to be silent.

- It serves the flesh to exert the will. It is difficult to relinquish the will.

Jesus had to win the Sonship-battle exactly where we do—in the will of his manhood.

He fought that battle on our behalf so that we too could become sons and daughters of yielding childship, so that we would have the courage, strength, and example to pray in our own unseen Gethsemanes, "Not my will but yours be done."

Jesus has birthed the possibility. But only as we sink to our knees in our own invisible Gethsemanes, whispering the sacred words with him, do we bring his childship-life alive within ourselves.

5
Obedience

*Command-obedience—God's mechanism
to grow sons and daughters*

A question too few Christians stop to ask is so simple one wonders why it is not among the first teachings of Christianity 101:

What is the *primary* means by which the essential message of the Bible comes to us?

How many different answers would a random group of Christians give to that question? In reality there is a single answer.

The message of the Bible comes to us primarily by *command*.

It is not the *only* way God reveals his truth in the Bible. But it is his most *important* method of revelation.

LIFE'S ORIGIN— COMMAND ISSUED BY AUTHORITY

The authority of God's universal Fatherhood works itself into life, and *sustains* life, by

50

command. This resounding truth explodes off the pages of Scripture in its first chapter.

Let there be...

Let there be...

Let there be!

The universe was created by Authority. Man was created by Authority. Those under authority are expected to obey that Authority. It is how the creation was established to function.

We may not like it. Modernism positively hates it and therefore repudiates it. Children often don't like it. But we cannot escape it.

Authority and command—not DNA or RNA or amino acids or carbon and nitrogen and hydrogen and oxygen—are the true building blocks of life. Life *began*, not by accidental electrical and chemical reactions, but by Authority commanding its will into the formless void of the empty cosmos.

Authority and *command*, and the *obedience* that links and energizes them, are the basic building blocks of spiritual chemistry and physics. The table of the elements of spiritual life contains only three elements. Everything is built out of authority, command, and obedience.

As we have seen, command is accompanied by free will. It is a two-sided coin. There are always two responses to command—obedience and disobedience.

To us has been given the power to *choose* whether to obey. We are free also to choose *not* to obey.

It is a curious state of affairs, that an all-powerful Creator, who loves the children of his making and who desires intimacy with them, would create those children with the capacity to turn their backs on him.

Yet this is where we find ourselves. Though we are the offspring of God's creation, we must *choose* to grow into his obedient sons and daughters.

Most men and women throughout history have chosen not to do so. The almost anarchist and often depraved lust for independence from authority that defines our time is ironically the result of the very gift God gave his human creation.

THE IMPERATIVE *IF*

This choice-component to the authority-command equation, especially in the Old Testament, explains why so many of the Bible's guidelines are accompanied by the simple word *if*. Such instructions are usually phrased as *if-then* propositions. They lay out two sides of the obedience coin, then spell out the inevitable consequences of obedience and disobedience.

No clearer example exists than in Moses' farewell address to the Israelites in Deuteronomy

30, with a final "command" whose *if* and its consequences are stark and clear.

> *"I have set before you this day life and good, death and evil. If you obey the commandments of the Lord your God which I command you this day, by loving the Lord your God, by walking in his ways, and by keeping his commandments...then you shall live and multiply, and the Lord your God will bless you...But if your heart turns away, and you will not hear, but are drawn away to worship other gods...I declare to you this day that you shall perish...I have set before you life and death, blessing and curse; therefore choose life, that you and your descendants may live, loving the Lord your God, obeying his voice, and cleaving to him; for that means life to you and length of days."* (Deut. 30: 15-20)

THE BIBLE'S EQUATION—COMMAND AND PROMISE

Many Christians focus largely for their scriptural diet on the promises of the Bible. Promises are categorized so that for every life-situation one can produce a corresponding promise to meet the need.

Many, however, do not live in the *reality* of those promises. They are *hoped for* and *prayed for* more than experienced.

The reason for this disconnect is that the Bible's promises are coupled to an overlooked scriptural equation. They do not exist in a vacuum. The Bible's promises are not free. They are linked by cause and effect to certain conditions. These conditions must be met before the promises can be fulfilled.

The promises represent the second half of a compound sentence. They occupy the "then" half of an "if-then" equation. Without the *if*, there can be no *then*.

The commands are scriptural if-hinges which open doors into the promises. As in the words of Moses above, promise is always linked to command. We see this *if-then* progression clearly throughout the book of *Proverbs*.

> **IF** *you accept my words and store up my commands within you...applying your heart to understanding, and*
> **IF** *you call out for insight and cry aloud for understanding, and*
> **IF** *you look for it as for silver and search for it as for hidden treasure,*
>
> > **THEN** *you will understand the fear of the Lord and find the knowledge of God...*
> > **THEN** *you will understand what is right and just and fair—every good path. For wisdom will enter your heart, and knowledge will be pleasant to your soul. Discretion will protect you, and understanding will guard you.*
> > —Proverbs 2:1-5, 9-11, NIV

This is surely one of the towering and majestic promises in the Bible. But its fulfillment is not automatic. The IF-hinge looms large.

The determinative IF explains why many do *not* walk in understanding, knowledge, wisdom, and discretion. They have filled their heads with knowledge, but they have not set themselves to become the kind of people in whom wisdom is able to flourish according to the first two chapters of *Proverbs*.

THE COMMANDED IF

The if-then equation is not neutral. *Command* is inherent in the IF. We are *commanded* to get wisdom:

Do not forget...Get wisdom; get insight. (Proverbs 4:5)

The *if-then* equation of *Proverbs* is usually easy to see. The *if-then* linkage in Moses' charge to the Israelites is equally clear. Many of the Bible's promises, however, are not phrased in such linear if-then statements. We have to search to discover the *command* or principle that governs the energizing fruition of a given *promise*.

It is always there. Some *command* stands as the root out of which every biblical *promise* grows. If we want the promise manifested, we must discover and live by the command attached to it.

The promise is the fruit. The tree that grows that fruit is the tree of command and obedience.

HOW WISDOM GROWS

God's commands to man proceed out of his eternal will for the universe. He purposes for mankind to grow progressively capable of living according to his will. This we do first by obeying at the lower levels of command. From obedience to lower, specific, and straightforward commands (*Do this...don't do that*) emerges insight to perceive higher principles.

Obeying loftier commands and discerning still more advanced principles, wisdom gradually illuminates the heart and mind toward increasingly complex truths and mysteries in the economy of the kingdom, and ultimately the wisdom to see far into God's eternal purposes.

Obedience is the soil out of which such high understanding and eternal wisdom grows. As George MacDonald phrased it, "Obedience is the opener of eyes." [5]

Some of the principles of God's eternal will are difficult to apprehend when looking into the distant future. There is much within God's overarching plan that remains for eternity to clarify.

Other elements of God's will he *has* made clear. The general principles of work, wisdom, understanding, knowledge, selflessness, choice, foresight, growth, prudence, order, predictability, accountability, diligence, humility, and so on, can be seen throughout the book of *Proverbs*. It is literally a guidebook, an instruction manual, for discovering how to live the high and holy thing called God's Will in daily life.

---

5 George MacDonald, *Unspoken Sermons, Second Series*, "The Way."

In the commands of the Bible we unlock the revealed Will of God. Beyond all the history, theology, doctrine, and disputed questions, the commands reveal God's purpose for mankind. That purpose can only be illuminated into the hearts and minds of those who make it their life priority to *obey* those commands.

The commands represent the *energy* of spiritual physics. [F]

JESUS' BENCHMARK IDENTIFYING HIS FOLLOWERS

We've referenced several Old Testament sources where command-obedience illuminates God's purpose and intended pattern for life—*Genesis, Deuteronomy,* and *Proverbs* being the most prominent.

But the imperative of command-obedience rises to its highest significance in the New Testament—most notably and imperatively in the four Gospels. Over and over, Jesus both says and implies that to be his follower one must live in obedience to his commands.

He goes further. He says that one who does *not* live by his commands—however correct may be his or her belief, however active in church, no matter that such a one may call himself "Christian"—such individuals are *not* his followers at all.

It is an idea, straight from the mouth of Jesus, [6] that, if understood and heeded, would crumble the entire fabric of organizational, corporate Christianity.

MORE THAN INNATE GOODNESS— CHOSEN PURPOSEFUL OBEDIENCE

Many use the word "Christian" to mean mere "goodness" with no spiritual component at all. This misapprehension has dogged Christianity since its earliest days and is especially prevalent in our own time—that goodness, kindness, love, and the rest of the virtues are *in themselves* equivalent to the obedience we're speaking of.

It is true that goodness, kindness, love, and all virtues *are* good things. Goodness *isn't* as filthy rags as some evangelists quote Isaiah 64:6 to bolster a misreading of God's intent. Quite the opposite—those who are good and kind are honored by God.

In this sense, such men and women who want to live good lives fall in, almost by accident, with many of Jesus' teachings. Their life priorities coincide with much gospel truth. Though some may disagree, I believe that such individuals will indeed be honored by God for their goodness. Goodness is a good thing.

---

6 Matthew 7:26; 25:45-46; John 14:15, 21, 23; 15:10, 14.

But goodness, in and of itself, cannot be equated with the kind of obedience Jesus commanded of his followers. Gospel obedience, rather, involves a deeply *spiritual* and *practical* decision to order one's life by the commands of Jesus. It is a decision reinforced ten thousand times by the ongoing daily choice to do what he said *because* he said to do it.

Obedience means obeying specifically *because* Jesus commanded us to do certain things, and not do certain things…to think certain ways, and not think in certain ways…to respond in certain ways, and not respond in certain ways.

As good as virtue is, therefore, it does not alone rise to this high level of Matthew 7:24 obedience—hearing Jesus' words and *doing* them.

George MacDonald is blunt and unyielding:

> Ask yourself whether you have this day done one thing because he said, *Do it*, or once abstained because he said, *Do not do it*. It is simply absurd to say you believe…if you do not anything he tells you. If you can think of nothing he ever said as having had an atom of influence on your doing or not doing, you have…ground to consider yourself no disciple of his…if, after all, he say to you, 'Why did you not do the things I told you? Depart from me; I do not know you!'…
>
> You can begin at once…to *be* a disciple of the Living One—by obeying him in the first thing you can think of in which you are not obeying him. We must learn to obey him in everything, and so must begin somewhere: let it be at once, and in the very next thing that lies at the door of our conscience! Oh fools and slow of heart, if you…do not set yourselves to do his words! you but build your

houses on the sand. What have such teachers not to answer for who have turned your regard away from the direct words of the Lord himself, which are spirit and life, to contemplate plans of salvation tortured out of the words of his apostles...There is but one plan of salvation, and that is to believe in the Lord Jesus Christ; that is, to take him for what he is—our master, and his words as if he meant them...To do his words is to enter into vital relation with him, to obey him is the only way to be one with him. The relation between him and us ...can nohow begin to *live* but in obedience: it is obedience. There can be no truth, no reality...of atonement...that is not obedience. [7]

And he adds in fictional form:

"In my room, three days ago, I was reading the strange story of the man who appeared in Palestine saying that he was the Son of God, and...I thought with myself,— 'Have I this day done anything he says to me...Did I ever, in all my life, do one thing because he said to me *do this.*' And the answer was *no, never.* Yet there I was...calling myself a Christian...I have *not* been an honest man..." [8]

The words in the Gospel are stark: Unless one lives by making the commands of Jesus life's priority...he or she cannot be considered a *true Christian*. This is the Lord's benchmark.

Where this staggering truth leaves a majority of Christendom's churches, one can only imagine. That this majority, by this standard, is peopled

---

7   George MacDonald, *Unspoken Sermons, Third Series,* "The Truth in Jesus."

8   George MacDonald, *Thomas Wingfold, Curate,* Ch. 31, "The Curate Makes a Discovery."

with a huge majority of non-Christians is a fact that few of those churches will ever realize. That corporate Christendom is so blind to this reality makes it all the more devastating to Christianity's influence in the world.

JESUS' ASTONISHING CLAIM

Matthew 7:26-27 [9] represents but one of the astonishing statements made by Jesus that are ignored by the great number of churches purporting to be following his teachings. Three more passages deserve close attention, addressing precisely this illumination of Christendom's worldwide ineffectiveness. They do not come in the *form* of command, yet reveal the imperative of command. [10]

All Christians are familiar with Christ's Great Commission—his final charge to make disciples of all nations and take his gospel to the ends of the earth. What has gone undetected, however, is the roadmap he gave detailing exactly how this world-changing enterprise is to be carried out. Jesus told his disciples and followers throughout time specifically *how* to carry out the Great

---

9 "Every one who hears these words of mine and does not do them will be like a foolish man who built his house upon the sand; and the rain fell, and the floods came, and the winds blew and beat against that house, and it fell; and great was the fall of it."

10 Matthew 28:29; John 14:21, 15:10, 17:21.

Commission with maximum effect, and how to transform their own characters in the process.

His statement is absolutely remarkable. Yet it has gone almost unnoticed for two thousand years.

Imagine we were to randomly query a room of a hundred people who claim to be Christians, from a diverse spectrum of backgrounds and churches, and pose two questions.

- *One:* "What is the foolproof method for carrying out Christ's Great Commission that would *guarantee* success?"

- *Two:* "By what means will Christ's followers grow to reflect Christlikeness in their personal lives and receive the Lord's *Well done, good and faithful servant* at the end of life?"

Both questions have the same answer. There are not a variety of answers. There is *one* answer. All other responses might point to a host of good things. But they would be *wrong* answers.

What do we suppose would be the percentage of correct answers? We can almost be assured that the result would be a failing grade, especially in those of Christendom's churches filled from Sunday to Sunday—according to Jesus' standard—of non-Christians.

Would sixty percent answer correctly...fifty percent? It's doubtful it would be even ten percent. How could churches full of people who have not set themselves to live by Jesus' commands possibly know the answers to these eternally important questions?

THE GOSPEL'S PEARL OF GREAT PRICE

Or imagine being told:

"There is a simple prescription embedded in the heart of Jesus' teaching, overlooked, untaught in the churches, ignored by most pastors and all theologians, that will grow Christlikeness of character within you, *and* will fulfill the Great Commission in your life by the impact this powerful secret exercises on those with whom you come in contact."

Would not any true follower of Christ, any serious Christian intent on praying the prayers of Christlikeness and childship, do anything to discover that secret? Such knowledge would represent the treasure hid in a field, the pearl of great price, the ultimate goal of spirituality.

In truth, such a secret exists. It sits right in front of our noses.

In light of the Lord's remarkable but unnoticed instructions about exactly *how* to "make disciples of all nations" and *how* to grow Christlikeness of character, the astonishing thing is that for two thousand years, Christianity has been attempting to carry out that commission, and a minority of *Christ-ians* and a great majority of faithful regular-attending *church-ians*, have been attempting to live, by *different* means.

It is an unbelievable thing. Jesus told us, if we tapped into this powerful secret, that the world would come to know him. In response Christians down through the years have spent most of their efforts engaged in a myriad of other things that can *never* accomplish those high purposes.

Christendom has been ignoring the one thing that *will* effectively influence the world for Christ, and doing a thousand things that are guaranteed *not* to successfully evangelize the world even if we do them for ten thousand years.

Are we really so dense as to have been ignoring his straightforward formula for so long?

THE SECRET OF PERSONAL AND WORLD TRANSFORMATION—COMMAND OBEDIENCE

At last we are in a position to answer the two questions posed to the hundred hypothetical individuals. Both can be answered in four words.[11]

The answers are simply:

- The world will know Christ as sent from God as Christians *do what Jesus said.*

---

11 I believe these conclusions are powerfully, and unambiguously implied within the four passages of footnote #10.

- Christians will abide in Jesus and thus reflect Christlikeness in their personal lives as they *do what Jesus said.*

It's not rocket science. Jesus said with unambiguous clarity: Obey my teaching and the world will know that I came from the Father. Obey my teaching and you will become like me.

This is why his Great Commission contains the words, "...teaching them to observe *all that I have commanded you.*"

Not teaching them to study it. Teaching them to *do* it. Teaching them to do it by observed example.

It is not enough to ask *what* would Jesus do. That can be done by intellectual analysis, which is the great blindness and Achilles heel of Christendom.

We have to *do* what Jesus told us, by *choosing* to do it, because he *told* us to do it.

The example they will observe and learn from is yours and mine: *Go to the nations and teach and example how to do what I said.*

The Great Commission says nothing about proving Christianity true, analyzing its theology, getting people saved or confirmed or taking them to Bible study, urging them to join a church, or enjoining upon them a prayer that will ensure them entry into heaven.

He tells us to teach people to *do what he said.*

It may be time that we collectively ask whether the doctrinal machinery of Christianity's ideas and belief systems is working as a basis for living and spreading the Gospel of Jesus Christ. Might it be time to refocus instead on *doing what Jesus said?*

The true gold of the Gospel. The benchmark separating true Christians from pretense Christians. The treasure hid in the field. The pearl of great price.

Chosen obedience to the Bible's commands.

6

Life at the Center

Balancing the inner life of prayerful dialog and attentiveness to God's Spirit, with an integrated outer life informed by the Spirit and bearing fruit in wholeness of personhood

Since my early twenties—at the foundation and in the background of a busy and active life of marriage, family, business, writing, relationships, heartaches, joys, ups, downs, successes, failures, discouragements, disappointments, physical and financial challenges, and the steady advancement of age—I have spent my adult years praying to more fully understand, and seeking to live in what I call "life at the center."

In brief what I mean is a life grounded and informed by a Center of spiritual gravity, the true North of creation and personhood, anchored in God's being and eternal purposes for his people and his universe.

In practical daily reality it means thinking, behaving, and conducting myself in harmony and in step with what I perceive to be God's personal and internal purposes for me—the man I am and the man he desires me to become—lived *inwardly* in relationship with him and *externally* in relationship with those around me.

(And emphasizing yet again the all-important point—*attempting* and *praying* to do so.)

These may sound like vague, lofty and unrealistic ambitions—too heavenly minded, as the saying goes, to be of much earthly good. For me, however, it has been an intensely practical quest—lofty, yes, but very down-to-earth in the attempt to actually *live* with that overarching purpose at the forefront of what life means.

That practicality is more encompassing and complex than nebulously "living in God's will." That oft-used phrase can mean anything, or can mean nothing. The higher the spiritual principles, the fuzzier they become to the analytical mind, which is why so much spiritual teaching is impractical and divorced from real life.

I hope I will be able to explain some of the specifics of how I perceive "life at the center" *can* be lived practically—oriented toward, anchored in, and given meaning by that "spiritual Center of gravity"—in the daily ups and downs, ebbs and flows, triumphs and disappointments, and joys and heartaches of life as it comes to us. Or at least explain how I try to remain attuned to God's purposes and anchored in that Center in *my* life, even in the midst of the persistent failings, fallings, and forgettings that are part of it.

In a manner of speaking this may be the most elusive and nebulous chapter, of this small book.

The very idea of attempting to live at the center, core, foundation—in the *essence* of what walking with God and true spirituality mean—probes deep into regions each man and woman must prayerfully explore for himself and herself.

I cannot predict for anyone else the specifics of that progressive adventure with God into his individual Holy of Holies. I can only try to illuminate, in halting and inadequate speech, something of what I have seen through a glass darkly in the years of my *own* quest to discover that "center." The story of that quest, however, each individual has to write on his own heart.

THE INTERNAL AND EXTERNAL
"CENTERS" COMPRISING THE CENTER

There exist two "life-*centers*" in which I envision my spiritual being dwelling from day to day, year to year—one internal and one external.

I must reiterate that the phrase "dwelling from day to day, year to year" represents the goal, desire, and prayer, certainly not the 24/7 actual *reality*, which falls frustratingly short of that heart's desire!

When I speak of dwelling in these two centers, I speak as one hopefully growing by baby steps— relying on God's Spirit to supplement my stubbornly weak humanity with the grace and help of his transforming touch—and thus inching in that direction. In the day to day, I don't see much progress. I must continually trust God to make up the difference, and ask him to remind and exhort me to turn again, in the midst of my forgetfulness, to the Center of those two centers. As I set head to pillow every night, I am flooded with reminders of my inability to live in them as I would have liked. Thus again I pray, "Father, do your work within me beyond what I can do on my own...accomplish your purpose...continue to grow me into childship."

Such remains my heart's desire, my aspiration, and my prayer. In other words, I speak of these high things as a pilgrim, not a sage.

There could be many descriptions I might give to these centers. Two words serve as a beginning:

- PRAYER—the undergirding focus of *internal* centered living.

- INTEGRATION—the unifying *external* harmony between spiritual focus and personal character, evidenced by equanimity and balance in behavior, thought, relationships, outlook, motivation, and goals as they are lived in the world but not of the world.

As the two centers—an *internal* center of prayer, and an *externally* centered life of integrated character—flow and function in interwoven harmony, we begin to glimpse a faint image of what I call "life at the center."

One of my primary literary and spiritual mentors whom I mention frequently in my writings, Quaker Thomas Kelly (1893-1941), speaks memorably of the balance between the outer and inner, functioning simultaneously in the midst of an active life.

"There is a way of ordering our mental life on more than one level at once. On one level we may be thinking, discussing, seeing, calculating, meeting all the demands of external affairs. But deep within, behind the scenes, at a profounder level, we may also be in prayer...gentl[y]... receptive...to divine breathings.

"The secular world of today values and cultivates only the first level...But...the deep level of prayer and of divine attendance is the most important thing in the world. It is at this deep level that the real business of life is determined...

"Between the two levels is fruitful interplay... the religious man is forever bringing all affairs of the first level down into the Light, holding them there in the Presence, reseeing them and the whole of the world of men and things in a new and overturning way." [12]

---

12 Thomas Kelly, *A Testament of Devotion,* 1941, pp. 35-36.

The idea of ongoing communion with God's Spirit in what I have called an "internal center of prayer" is based on the belief and conviction—I consider it a *reality*—that God's Spirit lives and dwells inside us. With this foundational awareness, prayer is *internal*.

This is a shift in outlook from what is often taken for prayer—addressing an impersonal Almighty with rote and memorized prayers, pulpit and rosary and prayer-book prayers, formulaic and repetitive prayers, pray-after-me sinner's prayers, prayers written to sound good to listeners but not meant for God at all, prayers of superstition not faith, chanted unison congregational prayers, ritualized meal prayers, and stock "prayers for every occasion."

We are seeking rather an orientation based on interactive dialog and listening communion *inside* our own hearts with the Spirit of him who created us and who dwells within us.

This forms a contrasting perspective of prayer from the outflowing gush of words, words, words addressed *to* God, or for the benefit of those listening in a congregation, a group gathering, or around a meal table.

We are seeking a life of prayer established in *listening* not *speaking*.

In *quietude* not *talk*.

It is prayer that inhabits the realm of attentive silence where the whispers of God's "still small Voice" can be detected, rather than drowned out with incessant loud proclamations of *our* own voices detailing laundry lists to God to make sure he is aware of our every need.

It is true, of course, that many of the prayers I have mentioned are humble, sincere, and flow from hearts of brokenness and deep gratitude to God. Prayers of heartfelt thankfulness are among the most personal prayers we can pray. Prayed in the right spirit, public prayers, too, can call us to that spirit of thankfulness, and to the listening quietude out of which God's still small voice is able to speak.

Listening prayer is ever conscious of Jesus' words in Matthew 6:7-8: "And when you pray do not heap up empty phrases as the unbelievers do, thinking they will be heard for their many words. Do not be like them."

The Spirit of God dwells, not just out in the impersonal cosmos, but in the very center of our being. Life at the center focuses our attention, not toward heaven, but *inward into ourselves* where we dwell, in the center of existence, *with* him.

It is in that mutual center of our humanity which we share with our Father and Creator and Jesus, where we discover the *internal* half of "life at the center."

TWO PERSPECTIVES OF INDWELLINGNESS—
INVITATION AND IMAGENESS

As I did in Chapter 2, I feel another digression is important here. I do not like to break the devotional flow of such a deeply prayerful topic. However, there is much confusion and debate about the nature of what I call God's "indwellingness." I consider it imperative to clarify how I use the term. That meaning is foundational to understanding life at the center. Some readers may prefer to skip past this detour to the bottom of page 78.

Two basic views are held to describe how and why God dwells within the innermost hearts of the men and women of his creation.

Both are highly theological and have been written and preached about as much as any aspect of Christian theology.

ONE: God's Spirit dwells in every human being universally. Because mankind was created "in God's image," his fingerprint can never be eradicated from the human soul. God's Spirit is *there* in every man and woman of his creation, whether acknowledged or not.

TWO: Because fallen man cut himself off from God by disobedience, his Spirit no longer dwells universally in mankind. This "cutting off," this separation, is called *sin*. By this view, there are two humanities—one lost, one saved, one in whom God's Spirit dwells, and one in whom he does not dwell. God's Spirit—or the Spirit of Christ—thus dwells *only* in those who invite him back into their lives and choose to return to him and live by his principles. This return or invitation is viewed as taking place by any number of mechanisms or "plans of salvation" or church teachings. These methods are described in a multitude of ways— being saved, joining a church, inviting Jesus into one's heart, being born again, repenting of sin, accepting Jesus, trusting Christ for salvation, being baptized and confirmed, etc. The effect is the same whatever its theological explanation: turning or returning to God, through Jesus, as the Fathering source of life.

WAYWARD CHILDREN AND
OBEDIENT SONS AND DAUGHTERS

These two theological perspectives are not mutually exclusive. Truth is contained in both.

God's creating fingerprint remains in every human being. Man's fall could never remove it. The fall *did* indeed separate mankind from God and from the desire to live according to his commands, instructions, and purposes. But it did not completely, even in the midst of sin, remove the *in-God's-imageness* of mankind's intrinsic humanity.

It is true, therefore, that there are two humanities. In my view, both are yet part of God's universal family. In spite of the fall, he remains the Father of all mankind.

Diverging from binary *saved* and *unsaved* explanations, George MacDonald distinguishes the "two humanities" with the terms *children* and *sons and daughters.*

All human beings, he says, are God's created *children*, but most are wayward, rebellious, self-satisfied, and spiritually dormant children who care nothing for their Father or the principles by which he commands them to live. For these, God's creative and Fathering DNA lies inactive, asleep, unrecognized, unheeded, and thus not an intrinsic part of life.

Some of those children, on the other hand, choose to rouse themselves from their apathy and spiritual slumber, awaken to the reality of sin and their separation from God, and acknowledge God's Fatherhood in their lives. In spite of their fallen sin-nature, they choose to ally themselves *with* God and make themselves his obedient sons and daughters.

At some point in life, a desire rises within them—a change, an about-face, a crossroads—after which they *want* to live by his principles. By a decision of the will (call it what you will—repentance, yielding to Christ, accepting God's offer of salvation) they decide to orient the rest of their lives to wakeful, active, and responsive relationship with him.

It was this life as children of our heavenly Father that Jesus came to teach and example to humankind. He taught the way to return to God and make ourselves, not mere passive beings created in his image, but wide-awake, obedient sons and daughters living by his truth.

That's why Jesus is central to this salvationary process—he taught mankind *how* to wake up, *how* to confront and remedy sin, and *how* to return to its Father. His commands lay out the roadmap of that return into childship. That's why salvation comes *through* Christ. That's why he called himself *the way, the truth, and the life.*

Those who follow Jesus in returning to their Father make themselves Jesus' brothers and sisters and God's obedient sons and daughters—committing themselves to living by his commands, instructions, and principles as taught in the Bible. These are those who have invited both Father and Son, by whatever means, to become the ruling Guides and Masters of life.

Thus, though God's parental DNA lies deep in all men, in some it is active and life-directing, in others it remains quiescent, awaiting the invitation to full-life participation.

MacDonald explains it: "Because we are his children, we must become his sons and daughters."

The expanded passage at first sounds confusing—seeming to indicate that we are *not* his children but we *are* his children, that we are *not* his sons and daughters but we must *become* his sons and daughters.

MacDonald often uses odd linguistic juxtapositions to drive his readers beneath the surface of learned doctrinal formulas. I include this brief passage because it is imperative for us to lay hold of the deep meaning MacDonald intends. He phrased it in this way to force us to rightly divide the seemingly contradictory statements, and thus plunge into the depths of their life-changing import:

> "He is our father all the time…but until we respond with the truth of children, he cannot let all the father out to us; there is no place for the dove of his tenderness to alight. He is our father, but we are not his children. Because we are his children, we must become his sons and daughters. Nothing will satisfy him, or do for us, but that we be one with our father… Because we are the sons of God, we must become the sons of God." [13]

THE SPIRIT WITHIN—DORMANT AND UNRECOGNIZED…OR ACTIVE PRESENCE, GUIDE, COMPANION, AND SHARER OF LIFE

I engage in this mini-treatise of theology because central to understanding "life at the center" is the recognition that God's Spirit dwells

---

13 George MacDonald, "Abba, Father!", *Unspoken Sermons, Second Series.*

within. He is calling, wooing, and whispering...
inviting us to share life with him.

Thomas Kelly describes it:

> Deep within us all there is an amazing inner
> sanctuary of the soul, a holy place, a Divine Center, a
> speaking Voice, to which we may continuously
> return...It is a dynamic center, a creative Life that
> presses to birth within us...a seed stirring to life...the
> slumbering Christ stirring to be awakened...And He
> is within us all. [14]

The many doctrines and perspectives of
yielding, turning, changing, waking, choosing,
and repentant salvation are secondary to its
reality. The call upon humanity is universal—to
become sons and daughters of obedience by
turning from sin, waywardness, self-satisfaction,
and spiritual apathy, and sharing life with God
and his son Jesus in this inner region of being.

As one shifts directions in life *toward* God (in
some lives suddenly, in other lives gradually) and
says, "I want to wake from dormancy...I want you
to rule my life...I want to share my life with
you...I yield to your transforming work within
me," a sea change takes place.

Life turns on its axis.

Inviting his full participation in all facets of
existence, God's Spirit is energized out of
passivity into active vibrancy of motive-directing

---

14 Thomas Kelly, *A Testament of Devotion*, "The Light Within," p. 29.

Life, or if one prefers to explain it, "comes into us" in a new way.

Jesus is the door into this new life of communion with his Spirit and the Spirit of his Father. He says, "Behold, I stand at the door and knock. If anyone hears my voice and opens the door, I will come in to him." [15]

The binary *saved-unsaved, heaven-hell* imagery so central to Calvinist and similar theologies has created an inaccurate confusion about this awakening, this yielding shift in life-direction, this turning from sin, this chosen invitation for Father and Son to take over the reins of life, this opening of the heart's door.

It is not a matter of praying a certain prayer and being suddenly *saved from hell* and being given a *ticket to heaven.* Of all the simplistic explanations of Christianity, this has surely been one of the most damaging to a true understanding of God's purposes.

Salvation, rather, denotes the decision—energized by Jesus' life and death and given daily reality by obedience to his commands—to fall in with God's purpose on a life-path of becoming. Being *unsaved* may be static. But being *saved* is progressive.

We need not go more deeply into the theology of it than that. We who are engaged together in the prayerful quest to walk with God are mutually

---

15 Revelation 3:20.

committed to that purpose by whatever means our life journey has made us alive to that reality.

Understanding prayer as describing the inner, centering, listening, sharing of life with the Spirit of Christ and his Father on a life-path of becoming requires a shift in focus that bypasses many former preconceptions about prayer.

We are speaking of *active* engagement with that Spirit—listening, conversing, responding, and obeying the nudgings of God's still small Voice.

- Learning to listen, to hear God's Voice urging me to conduct my affairs according to his perspectives and purposes, influencing how I think, how I see people and the world.

- Obeying the soft whispers of the inner Voice and the leadings that emerge out of the silence.

- Seeking my Father's guidance, and submitting decisions to his direction.

- Training myself to see through Jesus' eyes, to see people and situations and all of life as he sees them, and then to respond as he would respond.

- Training myself to perceive God's eternal purposes for his sons and daughters, and translating that "becoming" purpose into the practical daily flow of life as his purpose for *me*…today…in the next five minutes.

This inner communion, I believe, anticipates with miniscule baby steps what Paul meant by the term "pray without ceasing."

One of the prayers I try to remember every day is simply this:

"What do you have for me today?"

Out of it flow more specific prayers:

- What do you have for me to do?

- What do you have for me to think?

- What do you have for me to focus on?

- What areas of gratitude would you remind me of?

- What insensitivities would you have me correct?

- Whom do you have to bring across my path?

- What do you have for me to write?

- What do you have for me to communicate to your people?

- What insights do you have for me into your purposes?

These prayers may seem at first somewhat self-centric, as "all about me." Prayer is clearly wider in scope and more comprehensive than that. Active prayer for *others* is drawn up into the listening quietude in which we are attempting to discern God's will and purposes in the hearts of *all* those whose lives intersect with our own. Lifting those we love through prayer into the Father heart of God flows as a unity out of the universal heart's cry Jesus exampled in John 17.

It is obvious to anyone who has made the attempt that it is impossible to maintain attentiveness to the inner whisperings of God's Voice with anything even faintly resembling continuity. I am scarcely able to engage in such listening responsiveness a ten-thousandth of the time.

But toward this center of communion we are growing, in anticipation of the unceasing oneness with God we will enjoy in eternity.

ENGAGING CONSCIOUS AND SUBCONSCIOUS

It is my conviction that I gain further approach to the high thing when I engage the subconscious mind along with the conscious.

When the conscious mind forgets, if I have pointed my conscious and subconscious together toward God's purposes, the subconscious, in a sense, is capable of taking over the internal communion with God at a level I am not aware of.

In the midst of busyness, schedules, relationships, distractions, frustrations, and daily work and responsibilities, the subconscious remains the inaudible active participant behind the scenes, keeping the rudder of my life-purpose pointed true and straight though I am not thinking about it every minute.

Kelly calls this center of inner communion and listening dialog a "subterranean sanctuary of the soul."[16]

I find it helpful, if I may use the term, to *program* my subconscious, telling it what to focus on when my conscious mind goes out of sight, say before I fall asleep. I give my subconscious its marching orders for the night, to prepare my conscious self for the next day. The term "directing the brain" is akin to what I describe as "setting the desires of the mind and heart Godward."

Can God work at such levels to carry out his transforming work? I believe the answer is yes—as long as I continually point my heart's desire in the direction of his purposes, and regularly reaffirm the commitment of my whole self to those purposes and the processes he uses to accomplish them.

This orientation of inner listening, communion, dialog, and obedience—carried out in both the conscious and subconscious—I

---

16 Kelly, *A Testament of Devotion*, p. 31.

believe, points in the direction of Paul's words of unceasing prayer.

Integration, the word encapsulating the second half of centered-living balance from page 70—energized and empowered by the inner life of prayer—is also a term whose deep meaning may not be immediately apparent.

Its definition is both simple and profound. It stems from the word "integer," which means *whole* or *one.* It is the mathematical term for a single *whole* number (1, 3, 469, etc.), as distinguished from fractional numbers (1½, 3¾, 469¼...1.5, 3.75, 469.25). The first and primary integer is the number 1.

In its simplest terms, integrity means *strong, whole,* and *sound.* Containing no blemishes or imperfections. A perfect "one." No fractions, no fragments. Nothing left over or out of place.

Integrity describes strength, soundness, completeness, both structurally (the foundation of a building), and personally (the substance of human character).

To "integrate," as I use it to describe the nature of our humanity, signifies *wholeness*—bringing all parts of our humanity, personality, temperament, goals, attitudes, motivations, and life purposes into *oneness.*

Such integration describes a man or woman whose entire being is a human picture of the number ONE. The many diverse components of individuality are unified in harmony and undivided consistency.

When applied to morals and personal character, integrity takes on its most powerful import. In that context it rises to express the composite structural *oneness* of virtue—without cracks, splits, or weaknesses that undermine integral fabric, strength, and moral fiber. The *integer* of character.

Consistency is the hallmark of such integration. Everything about an integrated man or woman points in *one* direction.

Thomas Kempis calls it being "united within...inwardly single-minded...well-ordered and disposed" within oneself.

A COMMITTEE OF DIVERGENT SELVES

The spiritual implications are enormous. Our inner selves are more split, unwhole, and fragmented than we care to admit. Most of us are not *whole* numbers. We are not pointed in *one* integrated direction.

In so many ways we are *fractional* numbers. And not simply because we are weak, growing, and imperfect human beings, though that is an obvious part of it. More worrisome is that we choose fragmentation over unity of selfhood.

We *choose* to compartmentalize the *Self* into a fractional collection of multiple *selves*. They live inconsistently according to distinctive priorities, goals, and motivations. They point in different directions and are regulated by different standards of thought, conduct, and outlook.

It is hardly surprising, then, that these multiple selves—all vying for their own autonomous slice of the composite whole person—present different images and personalities depending on circumstances. Their conflicting motivations rule in different arenas of life—one series of motivations in church on Sunday, another set of perspectives ruling through the week in the world of business or school or finance; one series of motivations in a family setting, another set of perspectives when with friends; one series of motivations in a Bible study, another when filling out taxes or submitting a resume and boosting the glow of one's accomplishments.

This is easy to see in the political realm where So-and-so's behind-closed-doors behavior is the very antithesis of the public persona he or she allows to be seen. Yet are we not all guilty of wanting to show "our best side" to the camera, hiding our warts and blemishes?

We accommodate ourselves to these fissures of inconsistency, hardly realizing to what an extent they weaken the structural fabric of who we are. Thus, integration of personhood is dying all around us.

Thomas Kelly pinpoints it exactly. He writes:

> "The outer distractions of our interests reflect an inner lack of integration of our own lives. We are trying to be several selves at once, without all our selves being organized by a single, mastering Life within us. Each of us tends to be, not a single self, but a whole committee of selves." [17]

These distinct selves are often in direct conflict, pulling us apart, fragmenting motives and choices.

Integration of character requires alertness, the courage of hard choices, refusing to heed the voices from the various internal committees shouting for attention, the courage to look with one's true self straight into the camera.

Wholeness of purpose, singleness of eye, constancy of motive—these are virtues of character strength hard-won in the trenches where decisions and choices are made.

WALKING IN BALANCE BETWEEN THE
INTERNAL CENTER OF PRAYER AND THE
EXTERNAL CENTER OF INTEGRATION

Returning to where we began, life at the center is thus comprised of both an *internal (prayer)* and *external (integration)* centering focus. Internal and external intermingle in harmony and balance with a single objective: Growth into Christlikeness.

---

17 Kelly, *A Testament of Devotion*, p. 114.

That's what walking with God is—modeling life after the life of Jesus, who walked in continual communion with and obedience to his Father. In his life we observe the perfect balance between the inner and outer Center of Being. Everything about him—internally and externally—was anchored in and flowed out of the eternal purposes of his Father.

The *internal* life of listening, responsive, attentive, and obedient prayer informs and integrates the *external* life of behavior, goals, relationships, motivations, and purposes.

Both together—in synchronization and balance, neither more important, both dependent upon and giving practical life to the other, equally receiving the life of God through the other—illuminate what is meant by a life lived in the center of God's purpose.

It is an inner orientation of prayerful attentiveness which produces an integrated wholeness of character and unity of personhood lived in the daily world of men.

Many images rise to my mind as I prayerfully ponder this great mystery of what it means to walk with God.

I envision the atom as a picture of inner and outer centering focus, an electron and proton orbiting in perfect balance and harmony around the Fathering nucleus that unifies and gives life to the whole.

I envision the warp and woof of a divinely designed eternal tapestry being created that will reveal the full meaning of our days on earth. Our internal and external lives are woven on different strands and with distinctive threads of many varied colors and hues, each of which in the end will be indistinguishable as the full grand masterpiece God has been writing on our lives is revealed in eternity, along with the white stones of our true names now known only in God's heart.

The reality of life is a single whole. The tapestry is one. [18] G

---

18 If I may intrude with a suggestion, I may be preferable that Endnote "G" be read separate from this chapter. While highly fascinating, the material in that Endnote is too analytical to be absorbed with the same devotional and prayerful mindset with which we respond to the living breathing life at the center we all must discover in our hearts.

7

Authenticity of Personhood

In integrated wholeness of life-purpose,
we are reproductions of our Originating Life

Authenticity might be considered synonymous with integrity, even as an outgrowth or fruit of integrity. They are indeed closely intertwined. Yet their nuances of distinction are noteworthy in moving us ever closer to a more thorough understanding of what it means to walk with God.

To lay hold of the character of a truly *authentic* man or woman, an increasingly rare trait in our time, it is instructive to look first at its opposite.

INAUTHENTICITY—POISON TO PERSONHOOD

In my book *Endangered Virtues and the Coming Ideological War*, I emphasized authenticity as one of the most seriously endangered virtues of our time. I pointed to the progressive political correctness of our culture as largely responsible for creating the *inauthenticity* of personhood that so defines what I fear characterizes a majority of modern men and women.

A vast population of generally honorable men and women are afraid to be themselves, afraid to say what they think, afraid to be diligent in life's corners, afraid to be genuine and honest and true, afraid to look straight into the camera and be seen for who they are.

They are so fearful of reprisals that they allow themselves to lay down the authenticity of being true to themselves in favor of saying and doing and believing what society forces them to assume they are *supposed* to say and do and think. No clearer image of modern man's *lack* of authenticity exists than political correctness.

There is a serious price to be paid for inauthenticity. Going along with the crowd sacrifices the freedom of one's humanity. True personhood slowly and inexorably dies from the poison of inauthenticity. *Fractional* personhood is not *true* personhood.

Yet the implications of inauthenticity are more deeply spiritual than political or cultural. By definition, inauthenticity and hypocrisy are one and the same—pretending to be other than what you are. Hiding your true self behind a mask. Showing a fake persona to the public camera.

In its starkest form, inauthenticity is hypocrisy...pretense...duplicity.

Whether that mask is spiritual (as it was for the Pharisees) or political correctness (as it is for many in our day), the result is inauthentic hypocrisy. [19]

TRUE TO OURSELVES

At last we reach the crux that reveals why authenticity is such a major and significant component of a life well-lived walking with God.

Authenticity strikes to the heart of what it means to be men or women of truth, who walk in truth, live by truth, regulate their perspectives and decisions by truth, and are ever seeking more deeply to understand truth.

An authentic individual is *true to himself* in every facet and corner of life—not always *talking* about it, but, drawing again on Kempis's phrasing, *inwardly united within oneself.*

Authenticity walks in oneness of personhood. No hidden places. No masks covering what we don't want others to see. No dangling fractional shards of character.

The synonyms of authenticity are striking— reliable, trustworthy, accurate, real, dependable, transparent. Such qualities of character reflect truth, reality, completeness.

Authentic = True.

---

19 I must emphasize that this is entirely different from the quietude of silence, keeping one's own counsel, and being circumspect about too freely sharing opinions. Such silence-virtues are repeatedly emphasized by Kempis. Authenticity dwells comfortably in life's silences and knows when prudence dictates keeping one's mouth shut.

Authenticity excludes even the *possibility* of falsehood or hypocrisy.

TRUE TO OUR ORIGINAL

The most piercing definition of authentic is: "Genuine, faithful to the original and of undisputed origin."

Our origin, and thus our "original," is God our Father.

He created you and me in his image. Jesus is the fullness of Godness in the flesh—God in the reality of manhood, the genuine image of his Father, the one fully complete and *authentic* Man. In all ways, he reflected his Father. He was not a copy. The original life was in him, and *was* him.

We have been birthed into the same life that was in Jesus. We are reproductions of him.

Unlike the art world, however, where only one genuine "original" exists, in the spiritual realm, copies of the original are also genuine.

I am a *genuine* reproduction of the originating life of the universe.

You are a *genuine* reproduction of the originating life of the universe.

We are *originals*, writ small, of the Life that created the universe.

Our origin is undisputed. Our life's calling is to be faithful images of the one Son, because you and I, too, are genuine sons and daughters of his Father.

An atheist might well be a good man or woman, and integrated of personality and character. While not dwelling in the *inner* center of being, he or she might yet evidence aspects of *outer* centeredness as a child who does not yet know his Father. These may be *good* people and worthy of respect.

Yet in spite of such apparent visible signs of wholeness, they have not yet stepped up into *full* authenticity of personhood. Not acknowledging or walking in relation with his or her originating Life, the completeness of authenticity has not yet risen to Christlikeness as life's defining purpose, and is thus not imbued with the originating Father-source of life.

Looking at the outer crust of goodness their lives seem to reflect, few would call them *sinful* children. Yet they are self-satisfied children—too self-satisfied to seek their Father. They have not yet set themselves on the path to grow and become his authentic, true, and genuine *sons and daughters*.

In that authenticity—true to the Original within us, and true to ourselves...whole, complete, real, and true—we are called to step into the fullness of our humanity, and walk with God.

8

Virtue

Choosing to live by virtue

Virtue is the fruit of walking with God. At the same time, living by virtue, practicing virtue, cultivating virtuous ways of thinking and behaving, grows us into people who *do* walk with God.

It is easy to think of "fruit" as passive. We are taught that the fruit of the Spirit emerges more or less automatically in the lives of Christians. But that is not the way it works.

The fruit of the Christian life is active, not passive. We *choose* to grow fruit. God's Spirit comes alongside that choice, and, in cooperation with our obedience, enlivens and gives life to that choice, and works the miracle of growth within us.

The man or woman dedicated to walking with God, therefore, chooses to live a virtuous life, and the fruit of virtue grows in his or her life.

We *choose* and God *grows*.

WALK WITH GOD BY CHOOSING TO LIVE
THE FRUITS OF THE SPIRIT

Paul's fruits of the Spirit in Galatians 5:22-23 are preeminent among the virtue-fruits evidenced in a life walking with God. These are *chosen* virtue-fruits. They don't just *happen*, we choose whether or not to live by them in the next five minutes...every day...all our lives.

- Love
- Joy
- Peace
- Patience
- Kindness
- Goodness
- Faithfulness
- Gentleness
- Self-Control.

WALK WITH GOD BY CHOOSING
TO LIVE LIFE'S VIRTUES

In the book mentioned earlier, *Endangered Virtues and the Coming Ideological War*, I identified many of these virtues, and in addition discussed the following, which we also *choose* to cultivate, *choose* to make priorities, *choose* to practice. These all reinforce yet again the underlying premise of this small book—that to walk with God we *choose* to walk with God.

- Common Sense
- Love of Truth
- Preparedness
- Alertness
- Discernment
- Civility
- Attentiveness
- Diligence
- Authenticity
- Honesty
- Respect
- Courtesy
- Courage
- Integrity
- Purity
- Silence
- Wisdom

WALK WITH GOD ALONGSIDE THOMAS KEMPIS

Thomas Kempis, in his *The Imitation of Christ*, lays out what I call a "Practical Primer of Maturity." Many of its imperative principles are incorporated into the discipleship prayer of the final chapter.

In the following directives Thomas gives us a practical, daily, working picture of what walking with God looks like. [H]

- Judge with inner eyes.
- Be united within yourself and inwardly single-minded.
- Conquer yourself.
- Do not be rash.
- Enquire willingly.
- Hear with silence the words of holy men.
- Keep company with the humble, plain, devout, and virtuous.
- Do not be too confident in your own opinion.
- Avoid the tumult of the world.
- Do not busy yourself with the affairs of others.
- Unlearn evil habits.
- Patiently bear with the defects of others.
- Amend your faults.
- Do not be idle or spend your time in talk.
- Be grounded in true humility.
- Live in simple obedience.
- Walk in love and patience.
- Live a life adorned with virtue.
- Renew your purpose and stir yourself up daily.

- Diligently set in order both the outward and the inward man.
- Fix your purpose every morning.
- Every night examine how you have behaved in word, deed, and thought.
- Meddle not with curiosities.
- Withdraw from speaking vainly and gadding idly.
- Seek silence and stillness to learn God's mysteries. Do not entangle yourself in the affairs of others.
- Order your thoughts and actions as if today you were about to die.
- Avoid in yourself what displeases you in others.
- Avoid small faults.
- Give yourself to inward things.
- Think what you are about.
- Turn all things to good.
- Be zealous of your neighbor's good.
- Live peaceably with hard and difficult persons.
- Make simplicity your intention.
- Make purity your affection.
- Seek only the will of God and the good of your neighbor.
- Diligently attend unto yourself.
- Keep silent concerning others.

- Consider what you are within yourself.
- Give no heed to the whisperings of this world.
- Listen for the Truth teaching inwardly
- Prepare yourself to receive heavenly secrets.
- Gladly receive the pulses of the Divine whisper.
- Do not let death take you unprepared.
- Fear nothing, blame nothing, flee nothing, so much as your vices and sins.
- Keep yourself gently at peace.
- Look to yourself and do not entangle yourself with business not committed to you.
- Walk inwardly.
- Do not be moved with every wind of fleeting words.
- Keep silence.
- Purify the eye of your intention that it may be single and right.
- Make your endeavor and prayer to be stripped of selfishness.
- Be inwardly master of yourself.
- Preserve grace in silence.
- Give attention to the Lord's words.
- Allow the Lord to teach you without noise of words, confusion of opinions, ambitions, or scuffling arguments.
- Discern between things visible and spiritual.

- Walk in simplicity.
- Do all things purely.
- Delight in what is plain and humble.
- Be kind-hearted.
- Pray for grace.
- Imitate Jesus and practice his life.

WALK WITH GOD BY WALKING WITH GOD

We walk with God by *being* these things, living and practicing these virtues, and heeding these wonderfully practical exhortations.

The virtues embodied in these instructions and exhortations which Kempis gave to the young fifteenth century priests under his charge represent not mere by-products or passive fruits of a life with God. I view these as Spirit-inspired required imperatives for all God's people— marching orders for every day.

To walk with God, we put one step in front of the other, and then another, and then another— conducting ourselves in the small baby steps of life as the kind of people who *do* walk with God, by walking in God's ways.

We walk with God by walking with God.

9

Becoming

*Who do I want to be…what kind of person
am I in the process of becoming…
what character am I building into myself
that will flower in eternity*

Everything in life is about direction—which way we're going. Most don't think about the directionality of life's growth. They take life as it comes. They are content to float with the current of circumstances and events and the people around them. Their ultimate destination in life is more accidental than planned.

The most important of all directions is that of character. Who am I and where am I going?

- What kind of *person* am I?

- Who do I *want* to be?

- What is my *character-direction*?

- What kind of person am I *becoming* by my life-choices?

In God's economy, *becoming* is everything. What are we making of ourselves? What lasting and eternal character are we building into the fabric of personality, behavior, attitudes, goals, and relationships?

The meaning of life, the very meaning of the universe, is defined by *becoming*. We have been given life by God for one purpose…to *become*.

To become people capable of knowing him—understanding his being and purposes…then stepping into those purposes and making his purposes our purposes…and thus growing as his sons and daughters.

To become God's sons and daughters is the reason we are alive.

DIRECTION MORE IMPORTANT THAN POSITION

The direction we are going on life's road matters far more than where we happen to be at any moment. We meet many in life who seem farther ahead in some ways, and others perhaps who seem behind in other ways. Those differences hardly matter, only the direction we are all bound.

Where are our faces pointed on the continuum of becoming? Are we growing upward toward walking-with-God sonship and daughterhood, or walking downhill in the opposite direction away from them?

Life is also full of pleasurable intersections with many with whom we suddenly find ourselves sharing what seems a genuine kinship of soul. These relationships feel as if they will go on forever.

Yet those sparks of friendship and closeness do not usually reveal much about life's direction. We only know that at a moment of time a bond of common humanity has taken place. These are indeed genuine connections to be treasured.

Yet how many of such crossings eventually fade? Gradually paths diverge.

Life moves. Life goes on. It slowly becomes evident that we were not moving in the same direction with the one we mistakenly took for a soul-mate, comrade, and lifelong friend. We simply happened to cross paths and share a few brief intersecting experiences or interests. But our life's *directions* were not coincident at all.

Walking with God is a verb. It is not static. It is a statement of motion and movement. Every next step placed in front of the last is pointed in a direction. Two walkers may arrive at the same point and pause for a rest, but their next steps may take them along different paths in their life journeys.

In his classic book *The Princess and Curdie,* George MacDonald notes that some men are on the way downward to become less true, others are on the way upward becoming more true. Speaking to Curdie, the princess says:

When you met your father on the hill tonight, you stood and spoke together on the same spot; and although one of you was going up and the other coming down, at a little distance no one could have told which was bound in the one direction and which in the other. Just so two people may be at the same spot in manners and behaviour, and yet one may be getting better and the other worse, which is just the greatest of all differences that could possibly exist between them. [20]

When we get to heaven there will be many surprises. All at once the direction every individual has been moving will be visible for all to see. Some have been moving all their lives toward becoming more fully God's sons and daughters. Others never stepped into that highest of life's callings.

DRIFT ALWAYS TAKES US LOWER

Most don't think about, nor even care, what their lifetime of choices are turning them into. They float wherever the current takes them. Their *walking* is robotic not intentional. It takes no work to drift. Even dead fish float downriver. People drift in character because it is easy.

Drift, however, always takes you lower. The current of a river never leads upward. It is harder to walk up a hill than down. If you don't choose

---

20 George MacDonald, *The Princess and Curdie*, ch. 8.

your associations wisely, the people around you will mold your character downward.

It takes hard work to climb upward in character, to say *No* to the downward drift of conformity in order to become a man or woman who will make God proud.

It takes hard work to *become* a man of stature and integrity, to *become* a woman of character and inner beauty.

It takes hard work to expend the energy, self-reflection, self-denial, servanthood, graciousness, kindness, and goodness that *becoming* requires.

It takes hard work to halt life's random downward drift. Authenticity and integration of personhood do not gradually define who we are without the daily decision to *become*.

It takes hard work to make an about-face and say, "I will no longer drift with the current. Henceforth I set myself to follow the high road, to grow straight and true, to *become* more than I am, to grow into a centered, integrated, and authentic man or woman God will be proud of."

THE TRANSITION—CHOOSING TO BECOME

It may be that God must wake us up before we set our feet on the path of becoming. He may have to use extreme measures to jolt us out of our lethargy, to shock us to the imperative of becoming.

Change is one of the hardest things in life. It is easier to sit in one place than climb the mountain. It is easier to live by familiar habits and patterns than change them.

It is often said that people don't change. But that is only because they *won't* change.

Change is hard work, especially character change. It is hard to get out of the river, swim to shore, and begin climbing up the mountain of righteousness.

An individual who makes that difficult transition, who sets himself or herself to *become*, has embarked upon an eternal journey that leads to the sonship and daughterhood of Christlikeness.

Walking with God always leads uphill.

BECOMERS AND THE SELF-SATISFIED

The process of becoming is a defining principle of my entire outlook on life. In every novel I write, I envision my characters on the continuum of becoming. Some are moving upward, some downward. Some are choosing to walk with God in more aspects of their lives, some could not care less about walking with God. Some sit in self-satisfaction. Some climb.

I view every person I meet through the same eyes of *becoming*. I see what they can and should be and become in God.

For over fifty years, though I know my sight is still as through a glass darkly, I have been trying to see life and people, myself and the world, through *God-glasses* as another of my author-mentors, Frank Laubach, once described it.

Limited as is my heavenly eyesight, I would do anything to help set one who crosses my path on the upward road toward character becoming. But in my experience, that is not a help most people want. Most are too self-satisfied to be hungry to *become*.

Foolish is the man or woman, and there are many such men and women, who think they can help others by telling them what they *ought* to do, giving unsought counsel to the *unhungry*.

Exhorting the self-satisfied and unhungry to eat, and telling them what they should eat, is useless.

This vain practice is a particular passion for those who substitute the attempt to fix others for their *own* becoming. Self-satisfied and unhungry themselves, they are full of ideas how everyone *else* should change.

In Kempis's words, it is more pleasurable to *meddle in the affairs of others* than to *amend their own faults*.

Thus we are surrounded on all sides by non-becoming, unhungry advice-givers who love to *entangle themselves in the affairs of others* and in *business not committed to them* rather than looking to themselves.

As MacDonald says, whose phrasing I borrowed above:

> Foolish is the man, and there are many such men, who would rid himself or his fellows of discomfort by setting the world right, by waging war on the evils around him, while he neglects that integral part of the world where lies his business, his first business-namely, his own character and conduct. [21]

Our business is to take heed to ourselves and walk with God. When he brings us together with fellow becomers who share that heart's desire, who are on that same eternal life quest, then indeed does a foundation exist for the fellowship of mutually-becoming brotherhood in Christ.

---

[21] George MacDonald, "Salvation from Sin," *The Hope of the Gospel.*

10
Discipleship

A full-life orientation and lifestyle anchored in the irrevocable commitment as a disciple of Jesus Christ to obey his teachings, follow his example, and, in the midst of human weakness, to reflect him to a watching world, thus growing with his help into sons and daughters of his Father and our Father

A DISCIPLESHIP PRAYER: WALKING WITH GOD
DISCIPLESHIP DEFINED BY HOW WE PRAY

I give myself this day to you. I acknowledge myself your son/daughter. I affirm my intent and desire to relinquish selfish motive, yield independence of spirit, and to abide in your will not my own. Remind me constantly of this affirmation. Keep me centered in the quietness of your perspective, renouncing the world's values, and oriented toward my eternal citizenship.

Imbue me with your wisdom. Reveal yourself ever more fully to my understanding. Whisper to me out of the Silence. Still my heart and brain to remain attuned to your Voice. Focus my senses within the Center. Awaken me every moment to the commands. Press and urge your words upon me. Bring your precepts continually alive to my consciousness.

Give me courage, meekness, and wisdom to model my attitudes, behavior, and life priorities after the Lord's example, eyes to see people as he saw them, and a heart to love as he loved. While being diligent in my duties, genuine of speech, humble of response, courteous of manner, and gracious in relationships, help me not to be so swept up in the urgencies, stresses, pains, distractions, anxieties, and annoyances of the day that I forget you.

By the infinite miracle of your timelessness, make right the hurts I have inflicted through the years. May eternal forgiveness flow to and from every person to whom I was less than I should have been. Soothe, heal, and bring eternal good from the insensitivities of my responses and words. May my repentance stimulate a flowering of healing with every individual my path of life has crossed. Glorify every exchange into a transformed eternal Now of reconciliation, that may add its piece to the great reconciliation of your universe.

Infuse me, Spirit of Christ, with your presence. Breathe into me, through me, and out of me this day in all my thoughts, responses, words, and interactions with others of your brothers and sisters of humanity, sons and daughters of our universal Father. May I be your hands and your mouth to all I meet.

✧　✧　✧

May the prayer of St. Francis regulate my outlook, and be unspoken on my lips in every exchange:

Lord, make me an instrument of your peace: where there is hatred, let me sow love; where there is injury, pardon; where there is doubt, faith; where there is despair, hope; where there is darkness, light; where there is sadness, joy. Grant that I may not so much seek to be consoled as to console, to be understood as to understand, to be loved as to love. For it is in giving that we receive, it is in pardoning that we are pardoned, and it is in dying that we are born to eternal life.

✧ ✧ ✧

With Thomas Kempis, I pray:

Incline my heart to the words of your mouth. Because I am weak in love, and imperfect in virtue, I have need to be strengthened. Visit me often and instruct me that I may be made fit to love, courageous to suffer, steady to persevere. Enlarge me in love. Let me be possessed by Love.

Make me a dutiful and humble disciple. Unto you I commend myself to be corrected. You know what is expedient for my spiritual progress. Do with me according to your will and good pleasure. Grant me to know that which is worth knowing, to love that which is worth loving, to praise that which pleases you most, to esteem that highly which to you is precious.

Strengthen me with heavenly courage, lest the old man get the upper hand. Grant me heavenly wisdom, that I may learn above all things to seek and to find you. Purify, rejoice, enlighten, and enliven my spirit.

You know what is best for me. Deal with me as you think good. Set me where you will, and deal with me in all things just as you will. I am in your hand. Turn me whichever way you please. I desire not to live unto myself, but unto you.

Remind me not to judge according to the sight of the outward eyes. Give me true judgment to discern between things visible and spiritual.

Help me not to be wise in my own conceit. Keep me united within myself and inwardly single-minded. May my endeavor be to conquer myself. Keep me from being too confident in my own opinion. Open my heart and mind to enquire willingly, and hear with silence the words of holy men. Send into my life humble, plain, devout, and virtuous brothers and sisters.

Remind me to flee from the throng and tumult of the world, and not busy myself with the words and deeds of others. Give me grace and persistence to unlearn habits that do not reflect Christlikeness. Make me strong by patience and humility. Keep me from idleness and spending time in talk.

Turn my eyes unto myself. May I focus my attention on amending my own faults, bearing with patience the defects of others, always weighing my neighbor in the same balance with myself.

Keep me grounded in true humility, living in simple obedience, and walking in love, patience, and virtue. Remind me to renew my purpose and stir myself up daily, searching into and setting in order both my outward and my inward man. Remind me to continually recollect myself, fixing my purpose every morning, and every night to examine how I have behaved in word, deed, and thought.

Keep me from speaking vainly and gadding idly. Remind me that in silence and stillness I learn of your mysteries. Keep me from busying myself in matters which appertain to others, and entangling myself in their affairs. May I live such that death may never take me unprepared.

Alert me to those things in myself which displease me in others. May I thus avoid small faults. Remind me to give myself to inward things, to turn all things to good, to be zealous of my neighbor's good, and to live peaceably with hard and difficult persons.

May simplicity be my intention, purity my affection. May I seek nothing but the will of God and the good of my neighbor. Keep me diligently attentive unto myself and silent concerning others.

Keep me from heeding the many whisperings of this world, and from listening to voices sounding without, but for the Truth teaching inwardly. Thus may I prepare myself for the receiving of your heavenly secrets, gladly receiving the pulses of your whispers into my heart.

May I fear nothing, blame nothing, flee nothing, so much as my own vices and sins. Keep me gently at peace. In everything, remind me to look to myself and not entangle myself with business not committed to me. May I walk inwardly and not be moved with every wind of fleeting words. Still my tongue that I may preserve grace in silence. Purify the eye of my intention that it may be single and right. May my whole endeavor and prayer be to be stripped of selfishness.

In every place and in every action keep me inwardly master of myself, attentive to your commands. Keep me from heeding the noise of words, confusion of opinions, or the scuffling of arguments. May I walk in simplicity, do all things purely, delight in what is plain and humble, and be kind-hearted.

O Lord Jesus, grant me grace to imitate you. Let me be filled with the knowledge and practice of your life. Transform me into yourself, that I might be made one Spirit with you. Let your will be mine, and let my will ever follow you. Grant that I may die to all things of the world. Grant me above all things to rest in you, and in you to have my heart at peace.

✧ ✧ ✧

With David I pray:

Search me, O God, and know my heart. Try me and know my thoughts. See if there be any wicked way in me, and lead me in the way everlasting. Incline my heart to your commands. Teach me your ways. Give me wise judgment and knowledge. Protect me from falsehood, keep my steps steady, let no sin get dominion over me. Create in me a clean heart and put a right spirit within me. May integrity and uprightness guard my life. Guide me, lead me, and help me walk in truth.

✧ ✧ ✧

With Paul:

May my love for my fellows be patient and kind, not jealous or boastful, not arrogant or rude. May I not insist on my own way, and never be irritable or resentful. May I not rejoice in wrong but rejoice in goodness and truth, bearing all things, believing all things, hoping all things, enduring all things.

✧ ✧ ✧

With Thomas Kempis:

May my love be active, sincere, affectionate, pleasant and amiable, courageous, patient, faithful, prudent, longsuffering, manly, and never seek my own. May I be circumspect, humble and upright, not attending to vain things, sober, chaste, steady, quiet, and guarded in all the senses.

✧ ✧ ✧

Draw me to dwell in the deep waters where contentment, gratitude, patience, modesty, and tranquility flow beneath disappointment, discouragement, heartache, frustration, and complaint. Develop Christlikeness of character within me. Show me what you have for me to do and think about today.

Remind me continually to return to the simplicity and serenity of the Centered Life through silence, attentiveness, love, obedience, and childship.

Not my will but yours be done.

Endnotes

A   Nearly all my devotional books I have written first for myself. They invariably begin with an attempt to understand God's heart and some aspect of my walk with him more deeply. The exhortations are to myself. The prayers—such as in my Commands books and in the last chapter of this book—are prayers I pray myself. My occasional use of the pronoun *you* is, as it were, myself speaking *to* myself rather than trying to instruct anyone else.

Later, if I feel others might benefit from my prayerful explorations, I may make such writings available, though some of these personal writings have never been read by anyone else.

That has been the case here. It began with a personal quest to understand what I want to comprise the heart and focus of *my* walk with God. Converting my initial reflections into the language of "author to reader" should not imply that I suppose myself qualified to teach on these high things. I am ever conscious of the Lord's command in Matthew 23:10. I make those changes only for the benefit of some who may find my thoughts helpful in their lives of growth. If there are such who chance to read these thoughts, that is an added bonus to my initial purpose, and I will be glad.

B   After completing this small volume, I began reading a most intriguing book sent me by a dear friend, *Physics and Vertical Causation* by renowned philosopher-physicist and mathematician Wolfgang Smith (1930-2024). After a lifetime of work and numerous writings, the book was intended as a summation or overview of his long career. On the very first page of his Preface, he makes a statement remarkably similar to what I said on page 1 of my introduction. It so perfectly describes the purpose not only of his book but of my own that I feel it worthy of quoting here:

"My...objective is to bring into unity the multiple strands pursued in the books I have written over the years, in a way that manifests what may rightfully be termed the 'big picture.' I take the liberty, moreover, to express myself sometimes in broad sweeps, leaving it to the interested reader to consult this or that earlier work, where a more detailed and documented account of a particular subject is to be found. One has, in the evening of one's life, the luxury to speak freely, and focus on what constitutes the most ultimately profound fact of all. At that point 'lesser' facts hardly matter anymore in themselves. What counts in the end is an overview—like the panorama seen from a mountain top—in which everything finds its rightful place, and 'the many' mysteriously unite in that which is incomparably greater than their sum." (*Physics and Vertical Causation,* Wolfgang Smith, Angelico Press, the Philos-Sophia Initiative, 2019, pp. ix-x.)

Coincidentally Smith's career "summary" book is *exactly* the same number of pages as *Walking with God.* Perhaps 122 pages is just the right length in which to put one's life's writings into a focused perspective.

C   Grace as commonly taught in evangelical theology is usually defined as God's undeserved, unmerited favor, which is freely given and cannot be earned. It is associated with the "free gift" of salvation, from Ephesians 2:8—"For by grace you have been saved..." Whatever truth may be contained in such explanations, it is important to clarify how I use the word here. Grace in the New Testament is entirely a Pauline doctrine. It does not appear in the gospels. Jesus never spoke of grace and did not teach grace according to the above definitions. That it does not originate with Jesus no doubt accounts for the misuse of the term to bolster what I call the error of "passive sanctification" as being 100% God's doing. I use "grace," rather, to note the miraculous activity of the Holy Spirit that works *with* and *alongside* our obedience to effect personal transformation. God's grace accomplishes within us what we cannot bring about on our own, but it cannot do so without our willing, dedicated, and obedient participation in that process. This is *active* sanctification—a partnership between our obedience and the Holy Spirit. Or, using the analogy I have mentioned before, the two blades of a pair of scissors—our obedience being one blade, the transforming work of the Holy Spirt (or "grace") the other blade. Grace is not a *free gift,* it is the vigorous and forceful power of God's Spirit energizing our obedience unto Christlikeness.

D   Reading this manuscript, a close and lifelong friend whose wisdom I trust, succinctly articulated his reaction to these first two chapters, laying out briefly what is a more prevailing perspective than mine in evangelicalism. Because balance and objectivity are so important, I think it valuable to include some of his thoughts in order to emphasize again that the perspectives in this book are mine, and not all Christians agree with them.

My friend writes:

"I'm wondering if chapter two should be chapter one...I know you give a reason for this placement...Because I think belief (i.e. faith) is fundamental to the discussion your book prompts. We must remember that Paul was writing to believers in Corinth (regarding the love chapter, 13...And when Jesus said his disciples would be known by their love, he was, in fact, speaking to his disciples, not to unbelievers. Love was to be the fruit of salvation, not the way OF salvation. Jesus is the one who said "you must be born again." It seems to me all the commands are to be lived out as the fruit of saving faith...Consider one of my favorite verses, John 6:29, "This is the work of God, that you believe in him whom he has sent."...Another favorite verse is John 7:38, "Whoever believes in me, as the Scripture has said, 'Out of his heart will flow rivers of living water.'" What is the condition Jesus gives for living waters? It's belief in him. There are countless other verses that show that faith is the starting point in the Christian life...

"Regarding your opening of chapter one...a code of ethics, it seems to me, is an outer work that must spring from a deeper inner work. A person may adopt certain teachings from the Bible and build a code of ethics, but unless there's an inner work of grace, the foundation will be faulty....Jesus was very vocal about faith, believing, and trusting.

"You seem to minimize faith. All the 'do's' of Scripture, it seems to me, are a result of believing. The 'commands' as you call them are a result of believing. It's basically 'here's how a Christian should live and the power to live this life is propelled by the Holy Spirit.' Galatians 5 sets forth the fruit of faith. One cannot have Christian fruit apart from reliance on the Holy Spirit within.

"Also troubling is 'The heart of Christianity is not rooted in doctrine, theology, or belief...but in practical life as it is lived.' I believe the heart of Christianity *is* rooted in faith in Christ and evidenced by godly (and yes practical) living."

E   I hope none will mistake my not mentioning one or another doctrine (the nature of salvation, heaven, hell, the cross, the blood of Christ, repentance, the trinity, sanctification, and the other 90 or 100 doctrines some authors may consider "essential") to infer that I discount their significance. I reemphasize again that *all* the most significant doctrines of the Christian faith are included and drawn up into these three high overarching *truths.*

F   It is impossible in this small book to actually examine, list, or prioritize specific commands. Any to whom this book speaks I would encourage to follow with my "commands" titles. My lifetime study of the commands is presented in detail in: *The Bible's Commands, The Commands of the Prophets, The Commands of Jesus, The Commands of the Apostles, Principles of a Centered Life, A Book of Daily Memory Reminders, Jesus An Obedient Son,* and in the five volumes of *The Eyewitness Bible.*

G   I am compelled to quote again from Wolfgang Smith. His book, *far* over my head in spite of my degree in physics, if I understand him correctly, posits that "supernaturality" or "intelligent design," or *God* himself, can actually be akin to verified or *proven* by the observations and equations of higher physics. He says that conundrums, unanswerables, and observations of post-quantum-theory over the last hundred years *require* "vertical causation" from another realm than the purely physical, that some form of supernaturality is not merely a philosophical or metaphysical "idea," it is *required* to solve the "quantum enigma," which has remained unsolved for nearly a century. He literally infers a 'higher power" (i.e.—*vertical*) in the equations themselves.

In light of what I have written in chapter 6, however, I am most interested the following:

"But whereas," Smith writes, "vertical causality was discovered in the context of quantum measurement, it proves to be ubiquitous: nothing whatsoever can in fact exist without being 'vertically' caused…

"To comprehend…we need to understand…the cosmos at large…. There exists…a primordial iconic representation of that cosmos… consisting quite simply of a circle in which the circumference corresponds to the corporeal world, the center to the spiritual…and the interior to the intermediary. What needs to be understood—and may indeed be termed the 'hidden key'—is that…that center—that seeming 'point,' having neither extension in space nor duration in time, which appears to be the least—proves to be actually the greatest of all: impervious to the constraints of space and the terminations of time, it encompasses in truth every 'where' and every 'when,' and can therefore be identified as the *nunc stans*, the omnipresent 'now that stands.' Strange as it may seem so long as we picture it as something 'far away and high above,' that Apex is actually present within every being as its ultimate center. This means that every actual being is endowed with an ontological 'within' centered upon that Apex: it is as if the two centers actually 'touch.' [As the reader may note…that 'within' coincides with what the mystics are wont to call the 'heart'….]

"It is needful…to distinguish between the two centers: the one universal Center…and…the center of a particular being…." (*Physics and Vertical Causation*, pp. xi-xii.)

With his *nunc stans*, has Smith here identified Thomas Kelly's "eternal Now," and set in the nomenclature of physics the entire basis of my chapter on "life at the center? Perhaps my study of physics prepared me for a lifetime quest after "the center" more than I realized!

H   Some may wonder why I quote MacDonald and Kempis so frequently. It is because I believe to them was revealed many of the most significant elements of walking-with-God spirituality. Along with their insights, the Spirit of God empowered them to communicate in the words of their own times, and pass on those revelations with uncommon wisdom, insight, and practicality to their fellow sojourners. In writing of these things, I am but their humble follower, a seeker along paths they trod before me, one who is eternally grateful that they wrote down their insights to illuminate those paths for us who follow.

I also frequently quote Moses, David, Solomon, and preeminently, of course, Jesus. Yet I find it especially helpful and energizing to glean from ordinary men who faced the same challenges I do every day, men to whom God gave the wisdom to explain biblical principles in ways that help me live them more practically.

I esteem one of Thomas Kempis's injunctions in particular as among the preeminent guidelines for my life: *Hear with silence the words of holy men.* In my passion to pass on the wisdom of men who have influenced me, I recognize that I have not always maintained *silence* concerning what they have taught me. I am writing about them, after all, and encouraging their insights upon my fellow sojourners just as our brother Thomas did.

More of my thoughts, and many more excerpts from Thomas Kempis, may be found in my small booklet, *A Book of Daily Memory Reminders,* and from other of my life-mentors (including Thomas Kelly, who is also prominent here) in *Principles of a Centered Life.*

Made in the USA
Monee, IL
07 July 2026

56546308R00080